A Note From Rick Renner

I am on a personal quest to see a "revival of the Bible" so people can establish their lives on a firm foundation that will stand strong and endure the test as end-time storm winds begin to intensify.

In order to experience a revival of the Bible in your personal life, it is important to take time each day to read, receive, and apply its truths to your life. James tells us that if we will continue in the perfect law of liberty — refusing to be forgetful hearers, but determined to be doers — we will be blessed in our ways. As you watch or listen to the programs in this series and work through this corresponding study guide, I trust you will search the Scriptures and allow the Holy Spirit to help you hear something new from God's Word that applies specifically to your life. I encourage you to be a doer of the Word He reveals to you. Whatever the cost, I assure you — it will be worth it.

> Thy words were found, and I did eat them;
> and thy word was unto me the joy and rejoicing of mine heart:
> for I am called by thy name, O Lord God of hosts.
> — Jeremiah 15:16

Your brother and friend in Jesus Christ,

Rick Renner

How To Keep the Devil Out of Your Life

Copyright © 2019 by Rick Renner
1814 W. Tacoma St.
Broken Arrow, OK 74012-1406

Published by Rick Renner Ministries
www.renner.org

ISBN 13: 978-1-6803-1615-5

ISBN 13 eBook: 978-1-6803-1653-7

How To Use This Study Guide

This ten-lesson study guide corresponds to *"How To Keep the Devil Out of Your Life" With Rick Renner* (**Renner TV**). Each lesson in this study guide covers a topic that is addressed during the program series, with questions and references supplied to draw you deeper into your own private study of the Scriptures on this subject.

To derive the most benefit from this study guide, consider the following:

First, watch or listen to the program prior to working through the corresponding lesson in this guide. (Programs can also be viewed at **renner.org** by clicking on the Media/Archives links or on our Renner Ministries YouTube channel.)

Second, take the time to look up the scriptures included in each lesson. Prayerfully consider their application to your own life.

Third, use a journal or notebook to make note of your answers to each lesson's Study Questions and Practical Application challenges.

Fourth, invest specific time in prayer and in the Word of God to consult with the Holy Spirit. Write down the scriptures or insights He reveals to you.

Finally, take action! Whatever the Lord tells you to do according to His Word, do it.

For added insights on this subject, it is recommended that you obtain Rick Renner's book *Spiritual Weapons to Defeat the Enemy.* You may also select from Rick's other available resources by placing your order at **renner.org** or by calling 1-800-742-5593.

TOPIC

What Does It Mean To Be Sober?

SCRIPTURES

1. **1 Peter 5:8** — Be sober, be vigilant; because your adversary the devil, as a roaring lion, walketh about, seeking whom he may devour.

2. **1 Thessalonians 5:6, 8** — Therefore let us not sleep, as do others; but let us watch and be sober. But let us, who are of the day, be sober, putting on the breastplate of faith and love; and for an helmet, the hope of salvation.

3. **2 Timothy 4:5** — But watch thou in all things, endure afflictions, do the work of an evangelist, make full proof of thy ministry.

4. **1 Peter 1:13** — Wherefore gird up the loins of your mind, be sober, and hope to the end for the grace that is to be brought unto you at the revelation of Jesus Christ.

5. **1 Peter 4:7** — But the end of all things is at hand: be ye therefore sober, and watch unto prayer.

GREEK WORDS

1. "devour" — καταπίνω (*katapino*): to drink or swallow down; to devour; to destroy

2. "sober" — νήφω (*nepho*): to be sober, not drunk; to be free from the deliriums, delusions, and hallucinations that may accompany drunkenness; to think straight, not like a silly drunk; to be free of silly thinking and, hence, able to have presence of mind and clear judgment, enabling one to be in control of his thinking rather than be controlled by urges, impulses, whims, and fluctuating emotions; to have one's wits about him; to be rational, the opposite of irrational; to be free from a drunken state in which one drops his guard and is more likely to give way to foolish behavior, unreasonable conversations, and detrimental decisions; to be serious minded

SYNOPSIS

In the Sixteenth Century, fortification walls were constructed in Moscow to protect its residents by keeping evil forces on the outside. These walls were built because the city — and all of Russia — had been attacked many times: by Genghis Khan and his grandson, by Sweden, by the Teutonic Order, by Napoleon in the year 1812, and then during World War I and World War II. However, Moscow's walls were so secure that parts of the city were never penetrated by any foreign aggressor. These walls were designed to keep the enemy on the outside, and that's exactly what they did.

There is also an enemy trying to penetrate your life, but you can build a strong barricade to keep those evil forces on the outside. This ten-part series will give you practical steps to keep the devil out of your house, your health, and your finances.

The emphasis of this lesson:

Being sober-minded in the last days will keep you from being devoured.

In First Peter 5:8, Peter describes the activity of the devil as he tries to get into our lives. At the time this verse was written, the apostle Peter was a very elderly man, and he was writing to impart very common-sense advice to the people of God about how to live. He said, "Be sober, be vigilant; because your adversary the devil, as a roaring lion, walketh about, seeking whom he may devour."

When you see the word "devour" in this verse, you probably visualize a lion devouring the meat of an animal that he has already killed. But the Greek word for "devour" is from the root word *pino*, which really doesn't mean *to devour*. It actually means *to drink*.

So this verse is the picture of a lion hovering over the carcass of a dead beast, but the meat is already gone. All that's left is the bones and the fluid of the animal, and the lion is hungrily slurping up those juices. Peter used this word to tell us what the devil wants to do to you and me. He wants to mess us up, maul us, victimize us, and take us down — not just to chew and devour us, but to so totally consume us that there's nothing left but our "juices," so he can *slurp up* what remains.

Be Sober

Any pastor could testify that he or she has seen lives that were consumed by the work of the devil. Very often, those things happened because a believer left a door open. And through that open door, the devil got into his or her life. This is so serious, and the potential for destruction is so real, that Peter began this verse by saying, *"Be sober."*

In the context of a satanic attack, what does that mean? The word "sober" is from the Greek word *nepho*, which means many things:

- to be sober or not drunk
- to be free from alcoholic intoxication
- to be free from the deliriums, delusions, and hallucinations that may accompany drunkenness
- to think straight and not like a silly drunk
- to be free of silly thinking and hence able to have presence of mind and clear judgment
- being in control rather than being controlled by urges, impulses, whims, and fluctuating emotions
- to have one's wits about himself
- to be rational as opposed to irrational
- to be free from a drunken state in which one drops his guard and is more likely to give way to foolish behavior, unreasonable conversations, and detrimental decisions

Simply, the word "sober in this verse means *to be serious-minded.*

There are six key verses in the New Testament where this word *nepho* is used. In First Thessalonians 5:6, the apostle Paul used it to describe responsible living in light of the Lord's coming. He said, "Therefore let us not sleep, as do others; but let us watch and be sober." Considering what "sober" means in the Greek, we could translate this verse, *"Let us watch and think clearly, not like silly drunks who drop their guard and make foolish mistakes."*

Paul used this word again two verses later (1 Thessalonians 5:8) when he said, "But let us, who are of the day, be sober...." This could actually be translated *"But let us, who are of the day, be clear and rational in our thinking."*

In Second Timothy 4:5, we find a third usage of this word as Paul urged Timothy to be very level-headed: "But watch thou in all things, endure afflictions, do the work of an evangelist, make full proof of thy ministry." That phrase "watch thou" is from the Greek word *nepho*, and that verse would be better translated, "*Keep your head on straight. Get a grip on yourself and think straight, not like a silly drunk.*" Although this verse was originally written to Timothy, Paul was prophesying that there would be a lot of nonsensical thinking in the last days, and we are actually seeing that today. Many people are irrational and no longer thinking straight. They're intoxicated by the spirit of the world. Their thinking is off course.

So for us, this verse means, "Don't be affected by the spirit of the age. Don't be intoxicated with the same thing that's intoxicating the rest of the world. Be free of the spirit of the age — the wrong thinking and the deception that is in the world."

Another use of *nepho* is in First Peter 1:13 which begins, "Wherefore gird up the loins of your mind, be *sober….*" This verse portrays a marvelous picture of sober thinking. In Roman times, when a runner ran, he would "gird up the loins" by grabbing the loose, dangly ends of his skirt and tucking them under his loin belt. Why? Because if he allowed his skirt to dangle while he was running, it could get caught in his legs, and it would hinder his race. So a good runner would tuck those loose ends under his loin belt so his legs could move freely. This verse is saying, "Grab all the dangling ends of your life — all your loose places, your distractions, and *everything* that would hinder your race — and get them out of the way so you can run freely and attain your goal."

Then First Peter 1:13 continues, *"Be sober."* The word "sober" could be translated this way: "Wherefore gird up the loins of your mind *and put away irresponsible and foolish thinking that leads to bad decisions. Think straight* — not like a silly drunk." Really, this verse is calling us to responsible living. Why? Because the Lord is coming again, and we have a race to run before He returns.

First Peter 4:7 is also a call to responsible living in light of Christ's soon return. It says, "But the end of all things is at hand. Be ye therefore sober, and watch unto prayer." That word "sober" is again the Greek word *nepho*, and the first part of this verse could be translated like this: "*Be free from the intoxications of life.*" Why? Because when a person becomes intoxicated, he drops his guard. It becomes a time of foolishness. He makes bad decisions, and bad things take place. This echoes our main verse in First Peter 5:8, "Be sober, be vigilant; because your adversary the devil, as a roaring lion, walks about, seeking whom he may devour." Throughout the New Testament — especially in Paul's and Peter's writings — the word "sober" is primarily used as a warning to get a grip on oneself and to think straight, not like a silly drunk.

STUDY QUESTIONS

> **Study to shew thyself approved unto God, a workman that needeth not to be ashamed, rightly dividing the word of truth.**
> **— 2 Timothy 2:15**

1. The Greek word *katapino* translated "devour" in First Peter 5:8 has its roots in the meaning "to drink." How does this truth help you see that verse differently?

2. Comparing the six key verses in the New Testament where the Greek word *nepho* is used (1 Thessalonians 5:6, 8; 2 Timothy 4:5; 1 Peter 1:13; 4:7; 5:8), how would you describe the spiritual mindset every believer should have? What does the application of this mindset look like in everyday life? What is one example of an *opposing* mindset?

3. First Peter 1:3 could be translated "Grab all the dangling ends of your life — all your loose places, your distractions, and *everything* that would hinder your race — and get them out of the way so you can run freely and attain your goal." What are three examples of "dangly ends" in your own life?

PRACTICAL APPLICATION

> **But be ye doers of the word, and not hearers only, deceiving your own selves.**
> **— James 1:22**

1. Choose one of the three "dangly ends" you defined for Study Question #3 and develop a concrete plan to "tuck that end in." Then implement that plan and eliminate that habit, circumstance, or thought that keeps you from freely running your Christian race.

2. Whether it be a financial, relational, emotional, or other kind of situation, think of an area where you do not have your own "head on straight." Once you've identified that area, ask the Holy Spirit to give

you one verse that will help you think soberly about that issue and then meditate on that verse until it becomes a part of you.

TOPIC

What Does It Mean To Be Vigilant?

SCRIPTURES

1. **1 Peter 5:8, 9** — Be sober, be vigilant; because your adversary the devil, as a roaring lion, walketh about, seeking whom he may devour: Whom resist stedfast in the faith, knowing that the same afflictions are accomplished in your brethren that are in the world.

2. **Ephesians 4:27** — Neither give place to the devil.

3. **Matthew 24:42, 43** — Watch therefore: for ye know not what hour your Lord doth come. But know this, that if the goodman of the house had known in what watch the thief would come, he would have watched, and would not have suffered his house to be broken up.

4. **Matthew 25:13** — Watch therefore, for ye know neither the day nor the hour wherein the Son of man cometh.

5. **Matthew 26:38** — Then saith he unto them, My soul is exceeding sorrowful, even unto death: tarry ye here, and watch with me.

6. **Mark 13:34, 35, 37** — For the Son of Man is as a man taking a far journey, who left his house, and gave authority to his servants, and to every man his work, and commanded the porter to watch. Watch ye therefore: for ye know not when the master of the house cometh, at even, or at midnight, or at the cockcrowing, or in the morning. And what I say unto you I say unto all, Watch.

7. **Acts 20:31** — Therefore watch, and remember, that by the space of three years I ceased not to warn every one night and day with tears.

8. **1 Corinthians 16:13** — Watch ye, stand fast in the faith, quit you like men, be strong.

9. **John 14:30** — Hereafter I will not talk much with you: for the prince of this world cometh, and hath nothing in me.

GREEK WORDS

1. "vigilant" — γρηγορέω (*gregoreo*): to arouse from sleep; to be awake, as opposed to being sleepy and negligent; to be watchful, as opposed to careless and non-attentive; to give strict attention to; to be cautious; to be on high alert; to put up one's guard against a sinister outside force or enemy

2. "place" — τόπος (*topos*): any portion or space marked off, as it were, from surrounding space; an inhabited place, as a city, village, or district

3. "resist" — ἀνθίστημι (*anthistemi*): to resist; to arrange oneself against; to strategically oppose; pictures an orderly and planned resistance

SYNOPSIS

In Russian, the word "kremlin" means *a walled city* or *a fortress*. There are 26 different kremlins all over Russia, but *the* Kremlin is in Moscow, and behind its walls are the headquarters of the Russian government. In some places, the walls are 62 feet tall and 21 feet thick. Why would they build a wall like that around their headquarters? Because they wanted to protect it.

The Bible tells us that we need to do the same thing in our own lives. We need to build a wall of defense so strong that the devil can never find access into our personal affairs. Building that wall requires *vigilance*.

The emphasis of this lesson:

We must be on guard to protect ourselves from the enemy.

First Peter 5:8 begins, "Be sober, be vigilant." That word "vigilant" is from the Greek word *gregoreo*, which means *to arouse from sleep*. It is the picture of someone who is *awake as opposed to someone that is drowsy, sleepy, or negligent* — or *watchful as opposed to careless and non-attentive*. It implies *giving strict attention to something; being cautious and on high alert*. The best meaning of the word *gregoreo* is *to put up one's guard against a sinister force or enemy on the outside that's trying to get on the inside*.

By using this word, the Bible alerts us that there is a sinister force out there, and God's Word commands us — in fact, *it is our responsibility* — to construct a wall of defense that will keep that force from touching our lives.

Give No Place

Ephesians 4:27 also tells us to "give no place to the devil." That word "place" is from the Greek word *topos*, which describes a real, concrete geographical location. This tells us that the devil is looking for a concrete location, or entry point, through which he can access our lives and begin devouring us. This is why we must be *vigilant* to stand against his attempts to infiltrate our lives.

I want to give you an illustration from my own life. My wonderful wife Denise has always been a "fiend" about locking the door of our home! Moscow is a city of millions and millions of people, and when we lived inside the city limits, I understood her vigilance to secure the apartment where we lived.

But then we moved outside the city into a smaller community where we live now. Our house is on a piece of property with a big field behind it, and behind that, there is a forest. It feels like we're living in the country-side — at least by Moscow standards. However, after we moved outside the big city, Denise continued to lock the doors as if we were still living in downtown Moscow. I would often say, "Denise, I feel like we're living inside a *safe*. Before I walk out the door of our house, I have to unlock all of these locks!" Sometimes, I even made light fun of this habit of hers of securing every door in our house.

One day as I was watching television in our TV room, Denise *yelled* from the foyer of the house, "Rick, come here quick!" I jumped up and ran to the front door, and when I got there, she said to me, "Look out the peep-hole of our *locked* door."

I opened the peephole, and to my amazement, a naked woman was standing there! As it turned out, it was a woman on drugs. She had been in the forest, had walked across the field, and, because our back gate was open, came onto our property. She made it all the way up the steps to our front door and began banging on the door, demanding access to our house! We had to call a man to help us, and he came and put a blanket around her and walked her off the property.

Afterward, this dear woman stood just outside the back gate and lingered there, waiting for the man who helped us to walk far enough away so she could get back onto our property. He waited for quite some time to make sure she left, and eventually she did. She walked back across the field and disappeared back into the forest.

After all this happened, Denise looked at me and said, "Well, Rick, what do you think about that *locked* door?" And I realized, *Wow!* If that door had not been locked, it would have been a different situation altogether. I might have been watching the news only to look up as a naked woman walked through the door of our TV room! That would have been a scandalous situation. Not only that, it would have been difficult and clamorous — and perhaps even dangerous — trying to get her out of our house. It was so much easier to have the door locked and her on the *outside* than to deal with her after she had gotten on the *inside*!

My mind immediately went to Ephesians 4:27, "Give no place to the devil." In other words, the apostle Paul was warning us by the inspiration of the Holy Spirit to *close every door* and *seal every crack* of our lives. Then my mind went to First Peter 5:8, "Be sober, be vigilant...." In other words, we are to put up a wall of defense, and we're to do it very deliberately, *on purpose.* There's a sinister enemy who wants to find his way inside our lives to harm us. It is our responsibility to keep the doors of our hearts and lives locked and to put up a barricade to keep that enemy out!

Be Vigilant

The Greek word *gregoreo* is used in 12 key verses throughout the New Testament. In Matthew 24:42, Jesus used it to describe the attitude we must have about His coming: "Watch therefore: for ye know not what hour your Lord comes." The phrase, "Watch therefore" is *gregoreo* — the same word translated "vigilant" in First Peter 5:8. This particular verse in Matthew would be better translated, "*Therefore be on your guard. Something's going to happen. And if you're not alert — if you're not on your guard — it will take you by surprise.*"

Jesus continued in Matthew 24:43, "But know this, that if the goodman of the house had known in what watch the thief would come, he would have watched...." The word "watched" is also *gregoreo.* That part of the verse could actually be translated: "If the goodman of the house had known in what watch the thief would come, *he would have been on guard.*"

In Matthew 25:13, after Jesus had taught the parable of the ten virgins, Jesus said, "Watch therefore, for ye know neither the day nor the hour wherein the Son of man cometh." The word "watch" is again *gregoreo.* A better translation of the word "watch" here would be as follows: "*Stay wide awake and alert, therefore, for ye know neither the day nor the hour wherein the Son of man cometh.*"

And in Matthew 26:38, Jesus was in the Garden of Gethsemane when He said, "...My soul is exceedingly sorrowful, even unto death: tarry ye here, and watch with me." Again, "watch" is *gregoreo* and would be better translated in that verse as, "*Stay wide awake and alert — attentive — with Me.*" Jesus was calling on the disciples to be *vigilant*.

In Mark 13:34, Jesus was commanding us to be ready for His return. He said, "For the Son of Man is as a man taking a far journey, who left his house, and gave authority to his servants, and to every man his work, and commanded the porter to watch [*gregoreo*]." A better translation of the last part of that verse is, he "commanded the porter to *stay on guard and on alert, constantly watching.*" We also find *gregoreo* translated as the word "watch" in Mark 13:35 and 37. In these verses, *gregoreo* also implies an attitude of watchfulness, vigilance, and being alert and on guard. One expositor says it means *to be on HIGH alert.*

We also find *gregoreo* in Paul's words to the Ephesian leaders in Acts 20:31: "Therefore *watch*, and remember, that by the space of three years I ceased not to warn every one night and day with tears." In this context, this verse could be translated: "*Therefore, be on your guard against outside enemy forces and be constantly vigilant and on high alert.*" And in First Corinthians 16:13 when Paul said, "Watch ye, stand fast in the faith, quit you like men, be strong," the phrase, "watch ye" could once again be translated, "*Be constantly on alert and on your guard.*" It is very clear in Scripture that *gregoreo* always describes a state of alertness, of being aware that something could happen that could catch you off-guard. And that is precisely how Peter used the word in First Peter 5:8. "*Be sober, Be vigilant,*" is really a command for us to take responsibility to ensure the enemy never finds his way into our personal affairs, because he is "*seeking whom he MAY devour.*"

A Preplanned Method of Resistance

First Peter 5:9 continues, "Whom resist stedfast in the faith, knowing that the same afflictions are accomplished in your brethren that are in the world." That word "resist" is so very important. It is from the Greek word *anthistemi*, which describes *a preplanned resistance.* This is not describing a haphazard response to something that has happened to you; rather, it describes strategically building a wall of defense *in advance* that is so strong, so secure, and so thick that if the devil tries to attack, his attack will fail. By building a preplanned resistance, you do something on your part that stops him from finding entrance. Then it doesn't matter how hard the devil tries to attack, he will *not* get inside.

"Preplanned resistance" reminds me of the words of Jesus in John chapter 16, where He said to His disciples, "For the prince of this world cometh, and hath nothing in me."

These are very interesting words. First, when Jesus described the devil, He called him a "prince." Jesus knew that the devil had genuine authority in this worldly realm. Through deception, he took from Adam and Eve the authority that God had entrusted to them. However, despite that fact, he had *no* place in Jesus. Jesus was saying, in effect, "*He can come as often as he wants. He can circle Me, looking for a way to get in. But it will have no effect because he has no entry point in Me.*" Why? Because Jesus lived such a consecrated life that every door and window was closed, and every crack was sealed.

I believe in spiritual warfare and that we need weapons to deal with the devil, but *the very highest level of spiritual warfare is in living a consecrated and sanctified life* — a life that is lived so right, and is constructed so well, that there are no open places through which the devil can find entrance. Let that sink into your heart and mind! (We'll talk more about "resisting" the devil in Lesson 5.)

STUDY QUESTIONS

Study to shew thyself approved unto God, a workman that needeth not to be ashamed, rightly dividing the word of truth.
— 2 Timothy 2:15

1. Looking again at the definition of "vigilant" from the Greek, list four words that characterize spiritual vigilance? Choose one of those words and look up its definition in a dictionary. Is there an area in your life where you could apply this word to gird up your walls of resistance against the enemy?

2. Go through your Bible and highlight the ten key verses where *gregoreo* is used (Matthew 24:42, 43, 25:13, 26:38; Mark 13:34, 35, 37; Acts

20:31; 1 Corinthians 16:13; 1 Peter 5:8). Which of these verses stand out most to you, demonstrating the seriousness of practicing vigilance — wakeful, watchful attentiveness — over your life. Why?

3. Using Christ's life as an example, name some characteristics of a sanctified life. How does developing these characteristics protect a believer in Christ from the enemy?

PRACTICAL APPLICATION

> **But be ye doers of the word, and not hearers only,**
> **deceiving your own selves.**
> **—James 1:22**

1. On a scale of one to ten — with *one* being sleepy and negligent and *ten* being on high alert — how would you rate your overall spiritual vigilance?

2. What is one thing you can do to improve your level of vigilance over your life? Once you determine that one thing, ask the Lord for help and then begin to do it on a regular basis.

LESSON 3

TOPIC

How the Devil Seeks To Take You Down

SCRIPTURES

1. **1 John 4:4** — Ye are of God, little children, and have overcome them: because greater is he that is in you, than he that is in the world.

2. **1 Peter 5:8** — Be sober, be vigilant; because your adversary the devil, as a roaring lion, walketh about, seeking whom he may devour.

3. **Matthew 5:25** — Agree with thine adversary quickly, whiles thou art in the way with him; lest at any time the adversary deliver thee to the judge, and the judge deliver thee to the officer, and thou be cast into prison.

4. **Luke 12:58** — When thou goest with thine adversary to the magistrate, as thou art in the way, give diligence that thou mayest be delivered from him; lest he hale thee to the judge, and the judge deliver thee to the officer, and the officer cast thee into prison.

5. **Luke 18:3** — And there was a widow in that city; and she came unto him, saying, Avenge me of mine adversary.

6. **1 John 1:9** — If we confess our sins, he is faithful and just to forgive us our sins, and to cleanse us from all unrighteousness.

GREEK WORDS

1. "sober" — **νήφω** (*nepho*): to be sober, not drunk; to be free from the deliriums, delusions, and hallucinations that may accompany drunkenness; to think straight, not like a silly drunk; to be free of silly thinking and, hence, able to have presence of mind and clear judgment, enabling one to be in control of his thinking rather than be controlled by urges, impulses, whims, and fluctuating emotions; to have one's wits about him; to be rational, the opposite of irrational; to be free from a drunken state in which one drops his guard and is more likely to give way to foolish behavior, unreasonable conversations, and detrimental decisions; to be serious minded

2. "vigilant" — **γρηγορέω** (*gregoreo*): to arouse from sleep; to be awake, as opposed to being sleepy and negligent; to be watchful, as opposed to careless and non-attentive; to give strict attention to; to be cautious; to be watchful; to be on high alert; to put up one's guard against a sinister outside force or enemy

3. "adversary" — **ἀντίδικος** (*antidikos*): a lawyer who argues in a court of law; a prosecuting attorney; a prosecutor who argues vehemently against the accused; an accuser who attempts to bring a guilty charge against a person on the basis of information from past actions or deeds; an attorney who brings formal charges against the accused based on some legal violation

SYNOPSIS

In Moscow, there once stood a colossal statue of Felix Dzerzhinsky, and it stood in front of the KGB headquarters. Dzerzhinsky had been the leader of the secret police under Vladimir Lenin and had arrested thousands upon thousands of people. Many of these people were sent to the gulags, or prison camps. Others simply disappeared, ruthlessly killed on the orders of this man Dzerzhinsky. The Russian-speaking people viewed him as someone to be feared, and when the Soviet powers collapsed in 1991, the city voted to dismantle his statue and remove it.

In the same way, Jesus voted to dismantle and remove the devil's prosecuting powers in your life. The devil may try to take you down, but Jesus already dealt with him. The devil is the one who has already been taken down and removed. Now it is up to *you* to construct a wall so he can never get back into your life to take you down again.

The emphasis of this lesson:

The devil is looking for some loophole or a violation that you've committed, so he can find access into your personal affairs.

In the last lesson, we found that in First Peter 5:8, the word "vigilant" really means *to be on high alert* or *to build a wall, put up a barricade, and do everything you can to take preventive action against sinister outside forces.* Why? Because we have an adversary who "walks about seeking whom he may devour."

I have seen the kind of destruction the enemy has wrought in people's lives. The devil gets in because they don't respond correctly to an attack, and it begins to wreak havoc. Then the devil keeps extending his tentacles into other areas until finally their entire life is filled with destruction. This does not mean we should be afraid of the devil. First John 4:4 says, "Greater is he that is in you, than he that is in the world," and that is true! However, we're unwise if we fail to realize there is a devil in the world who wants to take us down, and we fail take precautions to keep him out.

How do we do that? By understanding his intent, his schemes, and his methods of operation. First Peter 5:8 gives us some understanding by calling the devil our "adversary."

The Role of the Adversary

The word "adversary" is the very unique Greek word *antidikos* — the usage of this word was well-established in the Greek culture of the First Century. It described *a lawyer who argued in a court of law; a prosecuting attorney who argues vehemently against the accused.* It also describes *an accuser or prosecutor who intends to bring a guilty charge against a person on the basis of information from past actions or deeds,* or, similarly *a prosecutor who brings formal charges against the accused based on some legal violation.*

Think about the work of a prosecutor; a prosecutor *prosecutes.* And how does he prosecute? He can't just bring random charges against a person; he has to have evidence. He has to have information of some past violation — proof that some law has been broken. With that information in hand, he can proceed to prosecute with the intention of taking the violator down.

We're going to look at four scriptural examples of this word *antidikos* in the New Testament. In Matthew 5:25, the word *antidikos* is used twice in one verse. Jesus said, "Agree with thine adversary quickly, whiles thou art in the way with him; lest at any time the adversary deliver thee to the judge…." Though the word is translated "adversary" here, a better translation of that verse might be "Agree with *the prosecutor* quickly, whiles thou art in the way with him; lest at any time *the prosecutor* deliver thee to the judge…." In Luke 12:58, when Jesus said, "When thou goest with thine adversary to the magistrate…," we see that same Greek word. This verse could be translated, "*When you go with your adversary, that is, the prosecutor who is bringing legal charges against you based on evidence of wrongdoing…."*

In Luke 18:3, Jesus said, "And there was a widow in that city; and she came unto him [the judge], saying, Avenge me of my adversary." Here, "adversary" (*antidikos*) describes, again, a ruthless prosecutor. We could read this as, "And there was a widow in that city; and she came unto him, saying, 'Avenge me *from the attacks of my adversary, who is ruthlessly trying to prosecute me and take me down.*'"

As we come back to First Peter 5:8, where Peter said, "Be sober, be vigilant; because your adversary the devil…," we could actually translate this verse, "Be sober; be vigilant — because your adversary the devil, like a *prosecuting attorney,* is *searching for some loophole in your life, some place of spiritual violation where you have broken a spiritual law.* And like a *prosecuting attorney,* he will try *to use that evidence to legally prosecute you and take you down.*"

That is so important! We've already seen that the devil is looking for some entry point into our lives. But here Peter has been so good as to tell us *what kind* of entry point the devil is looking for. He works like a prosecuting attorney, which means he will look for areas of violation — areas where you have done something wrong or violated some spiritual law. He will look for any loophole and use it to attempt to prosecute you and take you down.

You see, even though the Greater One lives in you, and you are secure in Christ, if you have violated a spiritual law, you've created an entry point through which the devil can enter into your life. That's why it's important to "judge yourself that we be not judged" (*see* Matthew 7:1; 1 Corinthians 11:31) and turn from any sin or wrongdoing in your life — *repent* — so you can give the adversary no legal grounds to prosecute or attack your life.

Six Common Areas of Violations and Entry Points

There are six common areas of violations that will produce entry points for the enemy. Two are in the area of financial mismanagement. In particular, I'm talking about credit cards and not paying your tithe.

What happens if you abuse your credit cards? You end up with a financial problem and a potential entry point through which the adversary will try to attack your life.

Some people think when a new credit card shows up in the mail that God has sent them an answer to their dilemma. They "charge" even more, *adding debt upon debt*! I'm not saying this to condemn anyone but, rather, to help strengthen the walls in his life that can keep the enemy far away. But the truth is, when someone abuses his credit cards, he has created an entry point. He has violated the rules of common sense, and the devil will use that entry point to dive into that person's finances.

Or how about not paying your tithe? That's violating a spiritual law too. The devil knows whether you tithe, and if you don't tithe, he'll use that as an entry point to try to bring a financial curse.

These are two potential entry points that can occur in a person's life, both in the area of finances. A third entry point could be a wrong diet. Again, I'm not condemning anyone here. I've struggled with weight gain a lot in my life. But the truth is, if you mostly eat fast food and food that is bad for you, and you eat at the wrong time of the day, you're going to mess up your body. You're going to gain weight. You're going to have chemical problems. You're going to have blood-pressure problems. Then you might cry out, saying, "The devil is after my health! I'm under such attack physically." But how did he get in there? He does not have authority in a person's life unless that person opened the door for the adversary to get in and begin to accuse, attack, and try to get a "conviction" to bring destruction.

Or how about simply not taking the time to physically rest and recover from the busyness of life? I have to confess that I've been guilty of this many times. The majority of times when I've become physically sick, it's because I have not taken time to rest and recover after doing a lot of work. And because I don't give my body time to rest and recover, a door is opened. I have to repent and close that door by giving my body what it needs in terms of rest and recovery as God intended.

For married people, a fifth example of a potential "violation and entry point" may be a failure to spend quality time with your spouse. You both may be busy all the time, and you've fallen into the habit of almost never talking to each other like you used to in the early days of your relationship. You never go out and just have coffee. There's no fellowship between the two of you, and then you complain that you're drifting apart. What happened? Really, it's common sense. If you don't spend time with your spouse, you're going to create a place — an access point — through which the devil can get into your marriage.

Or how about being inconsistent with your children? If you say you're going to discipline them, but you never, or rarely, follow through, your children will eventually stop believing you. On some level, they won't believe you'll do anything you say, and it will create a wrong attitude in them and a disrespect for authority. Then those disrespectful children most often grow up to be disrespectful adults. And parents wonder, "*How did this happen?*" It happened through some kind of a violation.

If you have violated some spiritual law, and the devil, your adversary or prosecuting attorney, is now wreaking havoc in your life, what should you do? Well, first, ask God for forgiveness. Confess that violation according to First John 1:9. Put it under the Blood. And once it's under the blood of Jesus, you have the authority to spiritually begin pushing the devil back out of your life!

Friend, God does not intend for you to be victimized by the devil. We all make mistakes. But through the act of repentance and because of the blood of Jesus, we can put it all under the Blood and be vigilant about the way we live. We can construct our lives on a solid foundation — in such a way that the devil stops finding access into our personal affairs.

STUDY QUESTIONS

> Study to shew thyself approved unto God, a workman that needeth
> not to be ashamed, rightly dividing the word of truth.
> — 2 Timothy 2:15

1. What is the Greek word that is translated "adversary" in First Peter 5:8? What are some other definitions for this word "adversary"? What does this translation from the Greek tell us about the way the devil operates?

2. Matthew 5:25 says to "agree with thine adversary quickly." In light of First John 1:9, what might that mean when the devil has evidence of a violation against you?

PRACTICAL APPLICATION

> But be ye doers of the word, and not hearers only,
> deceiving your own selves.
> — James 1:22

1. Pinpoint a specific habit you have in one of the six mentioned areas of violation (for example, eating too many sweets, not walking in love with your spouse, etc.) that has served as an entry point for the enemy to attack you. What concrete steps can you take to barricade that entry point? Write the steps down and begin to implement them.

2. Imagine that you've blocked the entry point you indicated above. What might that area look like one month from now? What about a year from now? Write down a vision for new blessing and freedom in that area of your life.

TOPIC

What Does the Name 'Devil' Really Mean?

SCRIPTURES

1. **John 10:10** — The thief cometh not, but for to steal, and to kill, and to destroy: I am come that they might have life, and that they might have it more abundantly.

2. **Romans 16:20** — And the God of peace shall bruise Satan under your feet shortly. The grace of our Lord Jesus Christ be with you. Amen.

3. **Revelation 9:11** — And they had a king over them, which is the angel of the bottomless pit, whose name in the Hebrew tongue is *Abaddon*, but in the Greek tongue hath his name *Apollyon*.

4. **Revelation 12:9** — And the great dragon was cast out, that old serpent, called the Devil, and Satan, which deceiveth the whole world: he was cast out into the earth, and his angels were cast out with him.

5. **Matthew 6:13** — And lead us not into temptation, but deliver us from evil: For thine is the kingdom, and the power, and the glory, for ever. Amen.

6. **John 8:44** — Ye are of your father the devil, and the lusts of your father ye will do. He was a murderer from the beginning, and abode not in the truth, because there is no truth in him. When he speaketh a lie, he speaketh of his own: for he is a liar, and the father of it.

7. **Matthew 9:34** — But the Pharisees said, He casteth out devils through the prince of the devils.

8. **Ephesians 2:2** — Wherein in time past ye walked according to the course of this world, according to the prince of the power of the air, the spirit that now worketh in the children of disobedience.

9. **Ephesians 6:12** — For we wrestle not against flesh and blood, but against principalities, against powers, against the rulers of the darkness of this world, against spiritual wickedness in high places.

10. **Colossians 2:15** — And having spoiled principalities and powers, he made a shew of them openly, triumphing over them in it.
11. **2 Corinthians 11:14** — And no marvel; for Satan himself is transformed into an angel of light.
12. **Ephesians 6:11** — Put on the whole armour of God, that ye may be able to stand against the wiles of the devil.

GREEK WORDS

1. "devil" — **διάβολος** (*diabolos*): one who strikes repetitiously; carries the idea of penetration or breaking through; to throw, as in throwing a rock
2. "prince" — **αρχοντας** (*archontas*): prince; refers to one who holds the first place or one who holds the highest seat of power
3. "Satan" — **Σατανᾶς** (*satanas*): the adversary; the devil; one who hates, accuses, slanders, or conspires against; an adversary

SYNOPSIS

A monument stands in Moscow for all the Russian people who had died in the past at the hand of evil governments. Those honored are the thousands no one remembers, but who were sent to prison or killed by evil leaders who then took their personal belongings. Truly, these leaders were examples of those who came to "steal, and to kill, and to destroy," like Jesus said in John 10:10.

That's also what the devil wants to do to you. He wants to find a way to take you down and totally undo you. But there is a way to resist him, and it begins by knowing who your enemy is.

The emphasis of this lesson:

As a Christian, you have to know your enemy.

As believers, we have more authority than the devil does. We've got the Word of God, the name of Jesus, and we can keep the devil under our feet! In fact, the only mention of the devil in the whole book of Romans — a book where every important doctrine is listed — is in the last chapter almost as an afterthought. Romans 16:20 says, "And the God of peace shall bruise Satan under your feet shortly." There he's pictured as being under our feet. And he *is* under our feet, because of the work of the Cross and the resurrection. However, he still tries to operate to "devour," as we've already seen in First Peter 5:8.

I don't like to focus on the devil, but he is real, and we have to use our brains and do what is right, or he'll find access into our lives. I remember one time many years ago, an American minister taught me a great example of doing right in order to avoid the enemy. I had picked up this minister and his wife at the airport, and he was sitting behind me as a passenger in the car. I didn't have my seatbelt on because, back in those days in Moscow, wearing a seatbelt was not required by law. But as we were driving along the road, I suddenly felt the seatbelt *whisk* around my body and sort of "slap" me in the chest! It was this minister slinging the belt over my shoulder to let me know I needed to put on my seatbelt.

I told him, "I don't have to wear a seatbelt. It's not a law here." And he said something I will never forget. He said, "Has nothing to do with the law. Has to do with *brains.*" Well, from that time until now, I use my seatbelt when I'm traveling. Why? Because it's just smart; it's a preventive action to ensure my safety.

17 Names for the Devil

All scholars of the Church, past and present, agree that we have an adversary who hates the gospel and who hates us. The devil's entrance into the life of a believer is allowed primarily through a believer's negligence. Our enemy, the adversary, slips in through some uncommitted, unrenewed area — a loophole or violation — and then begins to wage warfare against us. Rather than hide from this foe, we must turn our eyes to the Scriptures to see what God has to say about the devil.

In the Bible, there are 17 names, symbols, and types ascribed to Satan. Of those 17, two are devoted to Satan's insatiable desire to destroy and are found in Revelation 9:11: "And they had a king over them, which is the angel of the bottomless pit, whose name in the Hebrew tongue is *Abaddon,* but in the Greek tongue hath his name *Apollyon.*" The name "Abaddon" is the Hebrew equivalent of the Greek name "Apollyon," and both mean *to destroy.* You can be certain that demon spirits, over which Satan rules as a king, possess the same destructive nature as their master. They also operate according to the instructions Satan gives them as he sends them forth to destroy.

How about the name "Beelzebub"? This name was initially used by the Philistines of the Old Testament to describe the god of Ekron, and it literally meant "lord of the flies." Originally it was spelled "Belzebub," but as time progressed, the Jews altered the name to "Beelzebub," which added an even dimmer idea to this particular name, as "Beelzebub" means *"lord of the dung hill"* or *"lord of the manure."*

Why is that important? This clearly pictures Satan as the lord of demon spirits. Obviously, the Philistines looked upon demon spirits in the same way one would look upon nasty, dirty flies that bite, torment, and irritate. And by adding a twist to this particular name of Satan, the Jews revealed another very important characteristic of the devil. Just like nasty, dirty flies, both the devil and his evil spirits are attracted to manure or environments where rotting, stinking carnality pervades. This is the environment where Satan best thrives. So if you're living a carnal life, your carnality will send forth a wreaking smell that will attract demon spirits.

Then there is the name "Belial," which is of Greek origination and means *worthless*. Wherever it's used in the Old or New Testament, it describes something filthy and absolutely wicked. Much like the connotation associated with flies, this tells us that Satan is filthy and wicked.

And in Revelation 12:9, he is referred to as the "the great dragon [that] was cast out, that old serpent, called the devil, and Satan." It's clear from this verse that the terms "dragon" and "serpent" are used interchangeably in reference to Satan's twisted, demented, and perverted nature. By employing the use of both of these names, the Bible also presents the devil as a deadly, poisonous, ready-to-strike-and-kill creature.

No one was more familiar with Satan than Jesus, and Jesus called him the "evil one" as He prayed what is traditionally called, "The Lord's Prayer." In Matthew 6:13, Jesus said, "Lead us not into temptation, but deliver us from evil," but the original Greek there actually says, "Deliver us from the evil *one*." Jesus also called him a "murderer" in John 8:44 where He said Satan "was a murderer from the beginning." The murderous nature of Satan was first manifested in Genesis 4:8 when he inspired Cain to slay his brother Abel. It was also Satan's murderous nature that inspired Herod to kill all the babies in Bethlehem. We continue to see the devil's murderous nature in the deaths of millions of early Christian martyrs and still today where injustice is rampant. We see murder prevailing on the earth, and murder is a part of Satan's demented nature.

He's also called a prince. By calling Satan "the prince of this world," even Jesus recognized his temporal control over certain things in the earthly sphere. You might remember that, when Jesus was tempted in the wilderness, Satan himself personally offered Jesus the kingdoms of this world during those 40 days. In Matthew 9:34, Jesus also called him "the prince of demons"(*NIV*). The word "prince" here is taken from the Greek word *archontas*, and it refers to *one who holds the first place or one who holds the highest seat of power*.

Satan is also called "the prince of the power of the air" in Ephesians 2:2. The title "prince of demons" most assuredly reveals that Satan holds the highest-ranking seat among a host of diabolical spirits and that there is some kind of rank-and-file organization to Satan's system of governing his kingdom. This is in complete agreement with Ephesians 6:12, which states that under Satan's control, there are varying degrees of spiritually wicked power like principalities, powers, rulers of the darkness of this world, and spiritual wickedness in high places. But among all those varying degrees of evil power, he holds the first place.

We've already seen in First Peter 5:8 that Peter calls him "an adversary." But Peter also calls him a "roaring lion." Wow. What awe and fear the mighty roar of a lion strikes in the heart of man! However, in the case of the devil, his roar is more fearsome than his bite. Colossians 2:15 declares, "And having spoiled principalities and powers, Jesus made a show of them openly triumphing over them in it." By means of the Cross and the resurrection, Jesus Christ stripped demonic powers bare of the authority they once possessed. However this has not stopped the devil from trying to *sound* dreadful. Through his continual hassling of our thoughts, his insinuations about failure, his concoction of unrealistic fears in our souls, and his constant onslaught against our minds, Satan tries to beat us down into defeat. This constant roaring in our souls is just another attempt of the adversary to wear us out, wear us down, and then swallow us up.

The Bible also calls Satan "an angel of light" in Second Corinthians 11:14, where Paul writes, "Satan himself is transformed into an angel of light." This presents another clear picture of this mastermind manipulator. Satan disguises himself to be something that he really is not.

He's even called "the devil," which is taken from the Greek word *diabolos* — a compound of the words *dia* and *ballo*. The word *dia* means *through* and carries the idea of *penetration*. The word *ballo* is taken from the Greek word *ballo*, which means *I throw, as in throwing a ball or a rock.* When the two words are compounded, the new word depicts the act of repeatedly throwing a ball or a rock against something until it penetrates and breaks through to the other side. So in the name "devil," we're not only given the proper name of this archenemy, but also his mode of operation. His name means he is one who continually strikes, beating against the walls of people's minds over and over again until finally he breaks through and penetrates into their minds. This enemy of both God and man is also called "Satan," which is taken from the Hebrew word *shatana*, which means *to hate* and *to accuse.* This word is used more than 50 times in the Old and the New Testaments, and it also carries with it the ideas of slander and false accusation.

Again, our enemy Satan is known as:

- Abaddon (Revelation 9:11)
- Accuser (Revelation 12:11)
- Adversary (1 Peter 5:8)
- Angel of Light (2 Corinthians 11:14)
- Apollyon (Revelation 9:11)
- Beelzebub (Matthew 10:25; 12:24)
- Belial (2 Corinthians 6:15)
- Devil (Ephesians 6:11; 1 Peter 5:8; Revelation 12:9)
- Dragon (Revelation 12:9)
- Evil one (Matthew 6:13)
- Murderer (John 8:44)
- Prince of this world (John 12:31)
- Prince of the power of the air (Ephesians 2:2)
- Roaring lion (1 Peter 5:8)
- Satan (Luke 10:18)
- Serpent (Revelation 12:9)

It is because of this archenemy we've been describing that Paul wrote to the Ephesian church in Ephesians 6:11 and urged them to put on the whole armor of God. It's also why Peter wrote in First Peter 5:8 to be sober and vigilant! You see, the Bible tells us all about our enemy so we can study our foe. What nation doesn't study its foes? Any nation who would say, "Well we're not worried about the enemy. We don't need to know anything about the enemy," would be a stupid nation.

If you want to be secure in Christ, you have to use your brains. You have to know your enemy and you have to take preventive action to keep him out.

STUDY QUESTIONS

Study to shew thyself approved unto God, a workman that needeth not to be ashamed, rightly dividing the word of truth.
— 2 Timothy 2:15

1. What did you read in this lesson that will help you fortify yourself to keep the enemy on the outside of your life? Explain briefly how common sense and the use of your brain can be used to resist this spiritual foe.

2. Of the 17 names, symbols, and types ascribed to the devil, which ones would you consider most descriptive in terms of your own negative experiences with his attacks? Write down why and write how you plan to close the door to the enemy so that those past situations don't become repeat experiences.

3. Although Satan is a formidable foe, what do scriptures like Romans 16:20 and Colossians 2:15 teach you about your position regarding him?

PRACTICAL APPLICATION

But be ye doers of the word, and not hearers only, deceiving your own selves.
— James 1:22

1. Identify one thought or idea the enemy has hurled at you again and again. Has he been effective in penetrating your mind with this thought? What can you do to stop that recurring thought and its power over your life?

2. Using Romans 16:20 and Colossians 2:15, construct a simple confession. Make that simple confession a regular part of your prayer life and spiritual walk.

TOPIC

What Does John 10:10 Really Mean?

SCRIPTURES

1. **John 10:10** — The thief cometh not, but for to steal, and to kill, and to destroy: I am come that they might have life, and that they might have it more abundantly.

2. **Luke 3:16** — John answered, saying unto them all, I indeed baptize you with water; but one mightier than I cometh, the latchet of whose shoes I am not worthy to unloose: he shall baptize you with the Holy Ghost and with fire.

GREEK WORDS

1. "thief" — κλέπτης (*kleptes*): a bandit, thief, or scam artist

2. "steal" — κλέπτω (*klepto*): one so artful in the way he steals that his exploits of thievery are nearly undetectable; a pickpocket; it is where we get the word kleptomaniac

3. "kill" — θύω (*thuo*): not kill, as in murder, but to sacrifice; to surrender or to give up something that is precious and dear

4. "destroy" — ἀπόλλυμι (*apollumi*): to ruin, waste, trash, devastate, or destroy

5. "life" — ζωή (*zoe*): life filled with vitality

6. "abundantly" — περισσός (*perissos*): abundantly; excessively; exceedingly; extraordinary; something that abounds in an extraordinary measure; so profuse that it can be likened to a river overflowing and flooding beyond its banks; overflowing, plentiful, or even superabundant

7. "resist" — ἀνθίστημι (*anthistemi*): to resist; to arrange oneself against; to strategically oppose; an orderly and preplanned resistance

8. "stedfast" — στερεός (*stereos*): to bolster; to reinforce

SYNOPSIS

There is a park in Moscow, known in English as Victory Park, that was built as a memorial of World War II. Within the park, a special monument was built in honor of the Jews who died in the Holocaust. It is just unthinkable what happened to the Jewish people during that period. Millions of people of this race were slaughtered. The Nazi forces didn't just want to hurt them; they wanted to *liquidate* them as a people group. Yet the Jews survived as a people and are still thriving today.

Jesus said in John 10:10, "The thief cometh not, but for to steal, and to kill, and to destroy." That word "destroy" really means *to undo, to completely destroy*, or *to liquidate*. That's what the devil would like to do to you. But you do not have to be a victim. Even if he's already attacking your life, there's a way to push him back across the line. You can survive any attack and, in fact, do more than survive — you can *thrive* against a satanic attack!

The emphasis of this lesson:

The devil is a thief and destroyer, but God has different plans for your life.

Years ago, two sisters came to Moscow to attend our seminary. We loved these two dear women. They were involved in every area of the ministry, always joyful and smiling. But late one night, they were going home after seminary, and rather than walk across a bridge to cross the railroad tracks — which was the legal way to cross — they decided to perhaps save time by crawling through a hole in the fence below the bridge in order to cross the tracks.

Apparently, the women went through the hole, not realizing a train was barreling down the tracks. It must have come "out of nowhere" so quickly that they had no opportunity to retreat and no way to move away from the oncoming train. The train hit them, and by the time the train roared past the scene, there was nothing left of those girls' bodies but fragments.

People were stunned and began to ask, "How did the devil gain so much authority to destroy those girls?" As much as I loved those two sisters, the answer was very simple: They violated a very serious law for crossing those tracks, and it resulted in their deaths.

That's a very dramatic illustration. But if you look at your own life, you'll find that most of the places where the devil has attacked you have been in areas where you failed to do something you should have done — or you did something that you should *not* have done. That's where the devil looks to find a loophole. Jesus said when that happens, "The thief cometh not but for to steal and to kill and to destroy...." Thankfully, Jesus concluded by saying, "...I am come that they might have life, and that they might have it more abundantly."

The Thief

Jesus called the devil "the thief," which was translated from the Greek word *kleptes* — where we get the term "kleptomaniac." By using this word *kleptes*, Jesus was saying, "Don't be surprised. The devil can't help himself. He's flawed; he's defective. From the very beginning of time, he has been a thief. Something in him is bound and determined that he must try to take what belongs to someone else."

In the Old Testament, we find that the devil wanted the throne of God. He wanted the adoration of the angels, and he even wanted the geographical location of God's throne on the sides of the north. When we first see the devil working in the Garden of Eden, what was he doing? *Stealing*. He wanted Adam's position; he wanted the garden, and he wanted Adam's authority.

Jesus said, "The thief comes but for to steal...." The Word "steal" is akin to *kleptes*, the word for "thief." "Steal" was translated from the word *klepto*, the active form of the word *kleptes*. We could actually translate the first part of John 10:10, "*The kleptomaniac, when he shows up, will begin to behave like a kleptomaniac. He can't restrain himself. He'll steal, steal, steal just because it is his nature to steal.*"

An attack from the enemy may not even be about you. He just wants what you have because that's his nature. If you're healthy, he wants your health. If you're married, he wants your marriage. If you've got a good job, he wants your job. If you've got kids, he wants your kids. It doesn't even matter what it is; he just wants whatever is yours. And the word *kleptes* describes *a bandit, a thief*, or *a scam artist; one so artful in the way he steals that his exploits of thievery are nearly undetectable; a pickpocket*. When he shows up, he'll begin — very artfully and seductively — trying to take everything you have.

The Killer

Jesus continued to say that this thief comes to "kill." In the past, whenever I saw that word "kill," I always thought it meant slaughter, massacre, bloodshed, or murder. But then I looked at it in the Greek, and it's the word *thuo*, which doesn't mean murder at all. In fact, it's a religious word that means *to sacrifice, surrender, or to give up something precious and dear*. It was the same word that would have been used among the Greeks when they sacrificed to their gods — or even among the Jews when they sacrificed something to God.

In this word, Jesus is teaching us that the devil can disguise himself to sound very religious. This means if we've got anything left over after his stealing from us, he may try to speak to us in religious terms and say, *"You know what? There's no hope of recovery. There's no way you'll ever be able to restore what you've lost. Why try to believe? Just lay it all on the altar. You might as well give it up. Just sacrifice it and walk away."* He may even disguise his voice to sound as if it is God Himself telling you to lay everything on the altar. But this killer wants you to lay down your promises, your dreams, and everything dear that remains in your life so that he can continue his evil scheme to devastate and *obliterate* you.

The Destroyer

In John 10:10, Jesus also said the devil came to "destroy." That word is from the Greek word *apollumi*, the same root word used in Luke chapter 3 when John the Baptist said of Jesus, "...But one mightier than I cometh, the latchet of whose shoes I am not worthy to *unloose.*" Well, what happens when you "unloose" someone's shoes? Their shoes could become so loose that they begin to unravel and fall apart. That is the idea here in the Greek word *apollumi*. It describes something that is *ruined, unraveled, undone, devastated, trashed, destroyed*, or *completely liquidated*.

Pulling all of this together, my translation (RIV) of the first part of John 10:10 would read as follows:

> *The thief wants to get his hands into every good thing in your life. In fact, this pickpocket is looking for any opportunity to wiggle his way so deeply into your personal affairs that he can walk off with everything you hold precious and dear. And that's not all. When he's finished stealing all your goods and possessions, he'll take his plan to rob you blind*

to the next level by creating conditions and situations so horrible that you'll see no way to solve the problems except to sacrifice everything that remains from previous attacks. The goal of this thief is to totally devastate your life. If nothing stops him, he'll leave you insolvent, flat broke, and cleaned out in every area of your life. You'll end up feeling as if you're finished and out of business. Make no mistake. The enemy's ultimate aim is to obliterate you.

Yet Jesus said, "On the contrary, *I* have come that you might have life and have it more abundantly." That's the will of God for you! Jesus wants you to have life *and have life more abundantly* — life that is overflowing and spilling overs with a *flood* of blessings.

But the truth remains that the devil wants to take all he can from you, get you to give up all you'll surrender, and then take things to the next level to annihilate you. That's why you have to build a wall of defense and take a strong stand against him.

STUDY QUESTIONS

Study to shew thyself approved unto God, a workman that needeth not to be ashamed, rightly dividing the word of truth.
— 2 Timothy 2:15

1. Use the following method to compare the attributes of Satan and Jesus: Draw a line down the center of a blank page. Label one side "Satan," and the other side "Jesus." Using what you've learned so far in Lessons 4 and 5, fill in the left side of the page. Then, using a concordance or other resources, counter each statement with a corresponding attribute of Jesus. How does this listing more clearly help you define good and evil?

2. The Greek word *thuo,* translated "kill" in John 10:10, actually refers to a sacrifice. What does this tell you about the enemy's tactics? In what way have those tactics assailed your own life?

3. Find three New Testament scriptures that confirm the second part of John 10:10 — that Jesus came that we might have abundant life and write them down. Which one ministers to your heart the most? Why?

PRACTICAL APPLICATION

But be ye doers of the word, and not hearers only,
deceiving your own selves.
—James 1:22

1. Choose three different attributes from Study Question #1 that meant the most to you and write out a confession based on the following wording: "Although Satan tries to _____, Jesus _____." Remind yourself of these truths every time the enemy tries to approach your life to "steal, kill, and destroy."

TOPIC

What To Do if the Devil Has Already Gotten Inside Your Personal Affairs

SCRIPTURES

1. **1 Peter 5:8** — Be sober, be vigilant; because your adversary the devil, as a roaring lion, walketh about, seeking whom he may devour.

2. **Ephesians 4:27** — Neither give place to the devil.

3. **Ephesians 6:11** — Put on the whole armour of God, that ye may be able to stand against the wiles of the devil.

4. **James 4:7** — Submit yourselves therefore to God. Resist the devil, and he will flee from you.

GREEK WORDS

1. "submit" — ὑποτάσσω (*hupotasso*): one who is submitted to some type of authority; describes submission to authority in any context; to hide behind someone's back, showing that there is protection in submission

2. "resist" — ἀνθίστημι (*anthistemi*): to stand against; to stand in opposition; it demonstrates the attitude of one who is fiercely opposed

to something and therefore determines to do everything within his power to resist it; to stand against it; to withstand; to defy; militarily, it was used to depict a preplanned resistance; to arrange oneself against; to strategically oppose; an orderly and planned resistance

3. "flee" — φεύγω (*pheugo*): to take flight, to run as fast as possible, or to escape; it is the picture of one's feet flying as he runs from a situation; used to depict a lawbreaker who fled in terror from a city of nation where he broke the law

4. "stedfast" — στερεός (*stereos*): to bolster; to reinforce

5. "stand against" — ἀνθίστημι (*anthistemi*): to resist; to oppose or stand in opposition against; it demonstrates the attitude of one who is fiercely opposed to something and therefore determines to do everything within his power to resist it; to withstand; to defy; militarily, it was used to depict a preplanned resistance; to arrange oneself against; to strategically oppose; an orderly and planned resistance

SYNOPSIS

The walls of the Kremlin in Moscow are simply enormous. They're more than 7,000 feet in length, more than 62 feet tall, and up to 21 feet thick. Why did the Russians build such monumental walls? Because what was inside those walls — the people and the buildings — was precious, and they wanted to protect what was precious from the evil forces outside.

We also have to defend what's precious in our lives. Sometimes that means we need to have borders. We need to have restrictions. We need to do whatever is necessary to make sure the devil and all evil forces stay out — and sometimes that means reaching out to receive help.

The emphasis of this lesson:

When the devil has already found his way inside, you might need help to get him out.

It is better to keep the devil out than to deal with the devil after he has gotten inside. But what do you do if he has *already* gotten inside?

Sometimes the devil might get so entrenched in your life that you need someone else to help you get him out. Yes, you have the Word of God. You've got the power of the Holy Spirit. You've got the name and the blood of Jesus. But sometimes you have to humble yourself — especially when the devil has become so entrenched — and say to someone else, "Will you please help me?" And that other person or group of people, whether it is your pastor or a group of friends, may be able to take you by the hand and say, "Let me help you walk out of this attack, and let me help you construct a wall so this will never take place in your life again."

In Ephesians 6:11, the Bible says, "Put on the whole armour of God, that ye may be able to stand against the wiles of the devil." The phrase "stand against" — from the Greek word *anthistemi* — means *to resist and to push against*. It means with the weapons of warfare God gives you, you can push the devil back across the line. You can drive him out of your circumstances. You can push him out even if he was *entrenched*. But you may need help to do it.

The Bible tells us in James 4:7, "Submit yourselves therefore to God. Resist the devil, and he will flee from you." That word "submit" is from the Greek word *hupotasso*, and it describes *one who is submitted to some type of authority, one who is in submission to authority in any context*, or *to hide behind someone's back*. This shows that there is protection in submission. Sometimes that's what part of submission to God involves — submitting to someone else who helps you and prays with you.

Sometimes when you're in the middle of the war, and the devil is already securely entrenched in your life, you don't see things clearly. You need someone to help you see better and to take you by the hand and help you walk out of that mess. Maybe you need to hide behind somebody else's back who can help you deal with the problem — somebody else who stands with you and who prays with you so that the enemy cannot take what is precious to you.

STUDY QUESTIONS

Study to shew thyself approved unto God, a workman that needeth not to be ashamed, rightly dividing the word of truth.
— 2 Timothy 2:15

1. In James 4:7, the Bible says submission to God is the first step in fighting off the enemy. Find one or two examples of this truth operating in the lives of people in the Bible.

2. Choose three scriptures about overcoming the enemy. What do these scriptures tell us about ourselves? What do they tell us about God's protection and provision in our lives?

PRACTICAL APPLICATION

But be ye doers of the word, and not hearers only, deceiving your own selves.
—James 1:22

1. Is there an area in your life where the devil has already established a stronghold you can't overcome on your own? If so, pray and ask the Holy Spirit to show you where to get the help you need to get him out. Write down what the Holy Spirit tells you and pursue it.

2. Is there someone you know who is struggling with getting the enemy out of his life? Pray for that person and ask the Holy Spirit how you might be able to help the situation.

LESSON 7

TOPIC

How To Construct a Wall of Defense, Part 1

SCRIPTURES

1. **James 4:7** — Submit yourselves therefore to God. Resist the devil, and he will flee from you.

2. **1 Peter 5:9** — Whom resist stedfast in the faith, knowing that the same afflictions are accomplished in your brethren that are in the world.

3. **Psalm 5:3** — My voice shalt thou hear in the morning, O Lord; in the morning will I direct my prayer unto thee, and will look up.

4. **Matthew 4:4** — But he answered and said, It is written, Man shall not live by bread alone, but by every word that proceedeth out of the mouth of God.

5. **1 Thessalonians 5:17** — Pray without ceasing.

GREEK WORDS

1. "submit" — **ὑποτάσσω** (*hupotasso*): one who is submitted to some type of authority; describes submission to authority in any context; to hide behind someone's back, showing that there is protection in submission

2. "resist" — **ἀνθίστημι** (*anthistemi*): to stand against; to stand in opposition; it demonstrates the attitude of one who is fiercely opposed to something and therefore determines to do everything within his power to resist it; to stand against it; to withstand; to defy; militarily, it was used to depict a preplanned resistance; to arrange oneself against; to strategically oppose; an orderly and planned resistance

3. "flee" — **φεύγω** (*pheugo*): to take flight, to run as fast as possible, or to escape; it is the picture of one's feet flying as he runs from a situation; used to depict a lawbreaker who fled in terror from a city or nation where he broke the law

4. "stedfast" — **στερεός** (*stereos*): to bolster; to reinforce

SYNOPSIS

During World War II, the people of Moscow were so dedicated to defending their land, General Douglas MacArthur once said their resistance was the finest, most well-fought defense in the history of the human race. Likewise, to be sure your life is preserved if you come under attack, you need to be well-planned in your resistance of evil forces. You can't be happenstance about it. You must decide that you're going to put up defenses — that you're going to construct your life in such a way that the enemy will never be able to penetrate you, your family, your health, or your business.

The emphasis of this lesson:

There are practical things you can do to build a fortress — a wall of defense — around your life and make it very difficult, if not impossible, for the devil to find an entrance into your personal affairs.

James 4:7 says "Submit yourselves therefore to God. Resist the devil, and he will flee from you." That word "resist" is the Greek word *anthistemi*, which means *to stand against; to stand in opposition to.* It demonstrates the attitude of one who is fiercely opposed to something and therefore determines to do everything within his power to resist, stand against, withstand, and defy it. Militarily, *anthistemi* was used to depict a preplanned resistance, which I will discuss later in this lesson.

Here's something you need to know about the devil: As long as you do nothing to resist him, he'll push you here and there and all over the place. But the moment you resist him, guess what? He flees. The devil doesn't know how to take it when a believer resists him. The moment you say, "That's it. You're not pushing me around anymore. I'm going to move you," he's finished.

When you resist the devil, the Bible says "he will flee from you." The word "flee" is the Greek word *pheugo*. It means *to take flight; to run as fast as possible; to escape*. It was used to depict one whose feet were *flying* — or to describe a lawbreaker who flees in terror from a city or nation where he has broken the law, because he is fearful of punishment.

When you finally say, "That's it! I'm going to resist you strategically. I'm going to drive you out," the Bible says the devil will run like a lawbreaker who knows he's going to get in trouble unless he escapes. He will move his feet as fast as possible to get away from you when you begin to stand against him and resist. And you can do that because the Bible says you can.

We also see the word "resist" in First Peter 5:9 where Peter, speaking of this spiritual foe, says, "Whom resist stedfast in the faith…." Here "resist" is same Greek word *anthistemi*. But this time, it continues with the word "stedfast" — from *statheros*, a simple Greek word that means *to bolster or reinforce*, as in bolstering or reinforcing yourself.

Taking these two words together, my translation (RIV) of this verse would read:

> *Whom you must strategically oppose, resisting his potential assaults by putting up a preplanned resistance. You must do all you can to bolster and reinforce yourself in faith.*

This is not the picture of you saying, "Well, if I'm attacked, I'll figure out what to do then." That's foolishness. A smart person says, "I'm going to build my life in such a way that even if he tries to attack, it will have no effect on me." A preplanned resistance is bolstering and reinforcing yourself in faith so that even if the devil tries to get in, he can't. If he tries to assault you, it has no effect because you have a preplanned resistance in place that keeps him out. That's smart, and *that's* building a wall of defense to keep the devil out of your life.

Over these three final lessons, I'm going to give you a plan of resistance — seven ways to reinforce and bolster yourself in faith and build a solid wall of defense in your life. These are very practical things to do every day, and I'm going to speak to you directly from my own daily practices.

The First Brick of Defense: Every Day, Spend Time With God in the Morning

I can just hear someone say, "Oh, he's just going to talk about his daily devotional time" and not think this is very important. But if you're really serious about building a wall of defense in your life, I encourage you to do this each morning because the devil will try from the very outset to get into your day and your life. All you need to do is wake up to one bad email or text message — or have your spouse wake up in a strange mood, and the two of you don't quite hit it off right. Immediately, the devil will try to assault you. So how you start your day may determine whether or not you will keep the devil out of your personal affairs.

King David understood what it was to be assaulted. David had enemies in his home. He had enemies all around his kingdom. He was constantly being assaulted and tempted to struggle emotionally. All you have to do is read the book of Psalms to know that David struggled in his emotions. So David understood that when he woke up in the morning, the first thing he needed to do was lift up his voice to Heaven. That's why he said in Psalm 5:3, "My voice shalt thou hear in the morning, O Lord; in the morning will I direct my prayer unto thee, and will look up."

Of course, when you're directing your prayer unto God, you're directing your *thoughts* unto God. And that's why David said, "...And will look up." He'd learned early on that it was important for him personally to begin with prayer and *to look up*. If he didn't look *up* first thing every morning, chances were that he would begin to look *down*.

And it's the same for you. You have to make a deliberate decision: "Before I do anything else, I'm going to stop. I'm going to look up, and I'm going to direct my prayer to Heaven."

To do this every morning takes a serious commitment, but if you'll do what I'm telling you, you'll have peace. You'll feel confident. You will feel that you've done what is right. And you'll experience power to overcome the daily problems of life. But if you *don't* do what I'm saying, your emotions will continually be open to assault. You'll likely become very easily troubled. You'll be nervous and worried. You'll lack the spiritual power that is available to you.

When I talk about spending time with God, I'm not talking about spending hours in prayer every morning. Yes, it may require you to wake up a few minutes earlier. I encourage you to start before you even get out of bed — before you even lift your head off the pillow — and let God hear your voice. Direct your voice to Heaven. Begin by recognizing the lordship of Jesus over your life and dedicating your day to Him. If you'll do that, you will mentally be building a border — a barricade — that will keep the devil out of your emotions.

People often ask, "What do you do for morning devotions, Rick?" I'm telling you in this lesson what I do! When I wake up in the morning, before I lift my head from the pillow or before my feet hit the floor, I acknowledge the presence of God and Jesus' lordship over my life. That does not mean I lie in bed and have an intercessory prayer session. I do not. But I start my day by saying to Him, "Lord, this is Your day. I commit it to You right now. I recognize Your lordship. I'm asking You to direct my steps. I'm asking You to fill my thoughts. Father, I give this to You." It is a deliberate decision to begin my day by *looking up*.

Then I go to the kitchen. I get a cup of coffee. And when I have my cup of coffee, I go to my private place — which is a chair in our TV room — and I begin to read my Bible. And I let the Bible read *me*. As I read the Word of God, the Holy Spirit begins to speak to my heart. It is a very important time to me. In fact, it is such an important time that I have a self-imposed rule: No *Bible*, no *breakfast*! Not a morsel of food goes in my mouth until I've first taken the Word of God into my heart. Jesus said, "Man shall not live by bread alone, but by every word that proceedeth out of the mouth of God" (Matthew 4:4). Before I put any physical food into my mouth, I first take the Word of God into my spirit. From the beginning of my day, I have to be mentally *looking up* by doing these things, or I know an opportunity will likely come along to spoil my day.

Again, this does not mean you have to read your Bible for five hours every morning. But you *do* need to have a daily Bible reading plan that helps you take the Word into your heart. Not only will you feel a lot better and more confident as a Christian, that Word will nourish your heart. And as you read your Bible, I encourage you to include prayer. Let God hear your voice in the morning. Look up. Pray. Read the Word. Let it all be done together.

Again, I'm not talking about hours of reading and praying every single morning. Prayer is something you can do as you're reading the Bible, and it is something you can do on the go. The apostle Paul wrote in First Thessalonians 5:17 that we are to *pray without ceasing*. The Greek actually says, "Pray without a pause." It pictures a *lifestyle* of prayer.

In other words, pray as you read the Bible. Pray and ask the Holy Spirit to speak to you — that the words will mean something to you. Pray with your spouse. Pray with your children before they leave the house. Pray before you drive your car. Pray in the car. Pray before you get on a plane. *Just pray!* Make prayer something you do "without a pause."

When you do what David said in Psalm 5:3 — and what I'm suggesting to you today — you will build a wall of defense in your mind so that the devil will have a very difficult time penetrating your emotions, which is the first place he will try to strike. So make sure you build a wall in that area every morning to *keep him out!*

STUDY QUESTIONS

Study to shew thyself approved unto God, a workman that needeth not to be ashamed, rightly dividing the word of truth.
— 2 Timothy 2:15

1. Do a search for every time the word "morning" is mentioned in the Psalms. What do these scriptures say about God? About prayer? About life in general?
2. Ephesians 6:13, First Peter 5:9, and James 5:7 all talk about resisting the enemy. Using the five W's of information-gathering ("Who, What, Where, When, and Why"), write your own questions and develop Rick's ideas on wall-building from these verses.

PRACTICAL APPLICATION

> But be ye doers of the word, and not hearers only,
> deceiving your own selves.
> —James 1:22

1. If you don't already spend time with God every morning, take a few minutes to imagine yourself doing so in your daily routine. What challenges do you anticipate? How will you overcome them? Write it down and adjust your schedule accordingly.

2. If you already spend time with God in the morning, how can you make that time more meaningful for Him? Incorporate the answer to that question into your morning habit.

LESSON 8

TOPIC

How To Construct a Wall of Defense, Part 2

SCRIPTURES

1. **2 Timothy 4:13** — The cloke that I left at Troas with Carpus, when thou comest, bring with thee, and the books, but especially the parchments.

2. **Proverbs 27:19** — As in water face answereth to face, so the heart of man to man.

3. **Psalm 37:4** — Delight thyself also in the Lord: and he shall give thee the desires of thine heart.

4. **Psalm 46:10** — Be still, and know that I am God: I will be exalted among the heathen, I will be exalted in the earth.

5. **Hebrews 10:25** — Not forsaking the assembling of ourselves together, as the manner of some is; but exhorting one another: and so much the more, as ye see the day approaching.

6. **Psalm 54:4** — Behold, God is mine helper: the Lord is with them that uphold my soul.

GREEK WORDS

1. "resist" — ἀνθίστημι (*anthistemi*): to stand against; to stand in opposition; it demonstrates the attitude of one who is fiercely opposed to something and therefore determines to do everything within his power to resist it; to stand against it; to withstand; to defy; militarily, it was used to depict a preplanned resistance; to arrange oneself against; to strategically oppose; an orderly and planned resistance
2. stedfast" — στερεός (*stereos*): to bolster; to reinforce

SYNOPSIS

The massive Victory Park in Moscow, built in memory of World War II, is a reminder of how tragic war is so that it will never be repeated. One feature of the park are replications of the trenches that were built outside the city of Moscow, which were considered to be the most important fortification outside of Moscow against the Nazi forces. Grandmothers, children, husbands and wives — everyone physically able to carry a weapon or a shovel — went into the trenches to defend the city of Moscow. They understood that if they were going to survive, everyone had to be unified in their resistance against enemy forces.

In the same way, if you want to make sure the devil never finds entrance into your family, finances, marriage, or health, you — like those people of Moscow — will have to be unified in your stand against the enemy. You have to be very strategic. You can't just rely on luck or happenstance and hope that you won't come under attack. You have to be *preplanning* how you're going to stand against the work of the devil.

The emphasis of this lesson:

You build a strong defense every day when you spend time reading, being still, and connecting with those who strengthen you.

Looking again at this series' foundational scripture, First Peter 5:8, we are told, "Be sober, be vigilant; because your adversary the devil, as a roaring lion, walks about seeking whom he may devour." I want to draw attention to that word "whom." The implication here is that the enemy can't devour everyone, so he's seeking *"whom."* *That* person is one whom the adversary can devour.

The devil is looking for certain prey, just like a lion does. A lion doesn't attack the pack. He attacks the straggler — the one outside the pack — that is weak or sick. That's an easy one for a lion to devour. In the same way, the devil looks for believers who are not in fellowship — *stragglers*. These are believers weak in faith and spiritually sick. They are the ones who are easy to attack and devour.

When the Nazis came to Moscow, the people didn't just wait to see what would happen. They developed a preplanned resistance to make sure if the Nazis made it as far as Moscow, they would never get into the city. So the Muscovites went into the trenches. They built fortifications. They did everything required from their side to make sure the enemy never penetrated their borders and came inside.

And that's the attitude *you* must have in your stand against the adversary. You must, as Peter said, "resist stedfast in the faith" (1 Peter 5:9), or as I would translate it from the Greek: *"You must strategically oppose him, resisting his potential assaults by putting up a preplanned resistance. You must do all you can to bolster and reinforce yourself in faith."* And there are seven ways to do that — things you do every day. We already covered the first one: spending time with God every morning.

The Second Brick of Defense: Every Day, Spend Time Feeding Your Spirit on Other Sources

The second thing you can do to build a wall of defense every day is to feed your spirit on other sources than the Bible. This is so important. In Second Timothy 4:13, we find that the apostle Paul himself did this.

At the time Paul wrote this epistle, he was in prison in Rome about to be beheaded. And his last request was for *books*! He wrote, "…When thou comest, bring with thee…the books, but especially the parchments."

That verse is amazing to me because Paul was about to be beheaded. Very soon, he would see Jesus, and he would know everything. But he wasn't in Heaven yet, and he hadn't seen Jesus yet. So he still had time to read. He still had time to grow. It was as if Paul was saying, "In the short time I have left, I want to read. I want to feed my spirit. So when you come, bring me books."

Growing people are *reading* people. Stagnant people are not normally reading people. Reading is essential in order to grow. And reading good,

Bible-based books will feed your spirit. As fertilizer is to a garden, so is reading to your mind and to your spirit.

If you're not a reader, you can listen to CDs or MP3s in your automobile as you drive. I live in Moscow, an enormous city of millions, with as many as 30 million people traveling in and out of Moscow every workday. Because of that, we deal with an enormous amount of traffic. My youngest son drives several hours to work every day. But rather than waste the time he spends sitting in his car in traffic, he listens to audiobooks. He tells me all the time that he's reading books — "reading books" to him is listening to audiobooks. When he shows up at work, he is so filled with faith because he uses that time in the car to feed his spirit.

Think of how much time you waste driving in your automobile — time you could be using to feed your spirit. Or if you're a news fan, rather than watching the news nonstop every day, why not put some of your news time aside to feed your spirit on other sources that will cause you to be strong in faith? It takes time and effort to reinforce and bolster yourself so that what you're reading or hearing can affect the way you think in a positive way.

I personally listen to other preachers, and I listen to them a lot. In fact, when I'm finished at church on Sunday, I come home, sit in my chair in my TV room, turn on my computer, and go to different places around the world where I can listen to other people preach and teach. I need to do this regularly. When I feed on the Word of God — including the preaching and teaching of the Word — it makes me strong.

The Third Brick of Defense: Every Day, Spend Time in Quietness

It seems that some people are never quiet. They're just moving busily or robotically all day long without a pause. But quietness is very important for you to be strong in faith. People who are never quiet become dull and confused spiritually. A verse that I love says, "As in water face answereth to face, so the heart of man to man" (Proverbs 27:19).

One reason people get confused and come under attack is, they are no longer in touch with themselves. They don't know what they believe. They don't know what they need. They don't know what they feel. Instead, they just keep moving through life like a robot until finally they become numb to life itself. Much activity with no pause leads to spiritual dullness and confusion, and that is a very bad position to be in. People who become spiritually numb are susceptible to attack. It's not smart to allow yourself to fall into that condition. So I encourage you: *Don't do it.* You need some time of quietness every single day.

Quiet time doesn't have to be an hour at a time or even an hour out of your day. It might just be two to five minutes. Even the smallest amount of time being quiet will make a vast difference. All of us need deep contemplation to stay in touch with our own hearts. Psalm 37:4 says, "Delight thyself also in the Lord: and he shall give thee the desires of thine heart." But if you don't spend time with the Lord, and if you're not in touch with your own heart, how will you even know what your desires are or what to believe for? You won't. And very often, that's when confusion sets in. And where confusion is, the enemy works (*see* James 3:16). By staying in touch with yourself, you can help put up a wall of defense knowing what you feel, what you believe, what you need, and what you really desire.

You may not know how to find time to get quiet because your house is filled with kids, or you and your spouse are always together. Life can be so busy. But if you can't find any other place to go for a moment of quiet solitude, go to the bathroom, shut the door behind you, and lock it! Then capture that time as your moment to be quiet and still. If that's all the space you can get, take it as your time and place to be quiet in the presence of God.

Maybe your quiet time each day needs to happen during your lunch break at work. Or you might set your drive to work alone as your time of quietness. Another thing you can do is to get up before other people in the house are awake. That's what Denise and I do. We try to arrange our wake-up times so each of us can have a moment of aloneness to get in touch with our own hearts before the day gets busy. We truly incorporate this practice into our day to keep ourselves strong and avoid spiritual dullness. Our planning in advance to stay alert helps us keep the devil out of our lives.

The Bible commands us in Psalm 46:10, "Be still, and know that I am God...." It is a critical mistake to be constantly busy and never still. So every day, spend some amount of time in quietness. It will help you remain alert — and being alert helps you keep a wall of defense up so the devil doesn't mess up your mind and emotions and gain access to your life.

The Fourth Brick of Defense: Every Day, Spend Time With Those Who Strengthen You

You need to spend time with people who give to you — those who strengthen, bolster, and reinforce you. The Bible tells us in Hebrews 10:25, "Forsake not the assembling of ourselves together, as the manner of some is; but exhorting one another...."

I need fellow believers. Believers give me strength. Particularly, I need strong godly men in my life. And I have them. These are men who strengthen me. And every day, I spend some amount of time with those men who strengthen me.

This doesn't mean I have to have a planned appointment with every one of them every day. But I'm in touch with all of them daily by phone, Skype, or text-messaging. And it doesn't take long. In fact, sometimes it just takes seconds — sometimes it's just a text that says, "Good morning" to let someone know how I am doing. But every day, these men hear from me; and every day, I hear from them. We have a mutual relationship in which we exhort and strengthen one another.

These people also make for a wonderful kind of accountability — people who speak into my life and check on me when they don't hear from me. And not only that, they help me think straight if my mind is under attack or my emotions are under assault. I will say to them, "Please help me. I need to know whether I am thinking right or wrong about this situation." And because these are men who speak into my life, they've become like a safeguard. They might say to me, "Rick, this is not right" or, "Rick, you're thinking right — you're on track" or, "Rick, are you sure this is not a distraction?" This help from a sound, seasoned outside source is a great blessing to me.

These kinds of relationships are vital if you want to have a wall of defense that keeps the enemy out. When you're standing by yourself, it's much easier to come under assault. But when you have a united front standing with you, you become like a fortified wall that's very hard for the enemy to penetrate.

Many will say in response to this, "Well, the Lord is my helper." Yes, He certainly is. But look at the last part of Psalm 54:4: "Behold, God is mine helper: *the Lord is with them that uphold my soul.*" David said, "God is my helper. But how does He often help me? Through those around me who are upholding me."

Friend, we need people in our life who strengthen us. We need to be in touch with those who give us strength. And by the way, the men in my life I communicate with every day — those relationships didn't happen accidentally. They were built very deliberately. I made a decision to foster those relationships with people who could strengthen me. I need that, and so do you.

This reminds me of another monument in Victory Park dedicated to the international collective forces that fought against the Nazis. Standing side by side are four huge, bronze soldiers. First, there is a French soldier. Then there is a Soviet soldier. Then there is an American soldier. And then there is a British soldier. All of these forces cooperated during World War II because they had a common enemy. And to defeat that common enemy, they had to work together. You can perhaps win a spiritual battle by yourself, but it will be much harder. If you have others who can come alongside you and be your fellow comrades, *together* you can put the enemy to flight a lot faster.

STUDY QUESTIONS

**Study to shew thyself approved unto God, a workman that needeth
not to be ashamed, rightly dividing the word of truth.
— 2 Timothy 2:15**

1. Several scriptures admonish us to be still before God (Psalm 4:4, 46:10, 131:2; Isaiah 30:15; 1 Peter 3:4). According to these scriptures, how does God feel about stillness (quietness)? What benefits are there to being still before God?

2. Find at least three examples in the Bible of Psalm 54:4 — people the Lord used to help uphold someone else. Whom did they support and what was the outcome of their being called alongside that person to uphold him or her?

PRACTICAL APPLICATION

**But be ye doers of the word, and not hearers only,
deceiving your own selves.
— James 1:22**

1. Write a list of five books (other than the Bible) that will feed your soul in the things of God. Once you have a list, list the order in which you'd like to read them. If you don't have these books, find out how you can borrow them. The local library, online and digital sources, friends, and even your pastor might all be good sources.

2. Think of people who are spiritually strong and can, or do, speak into your life on a regular basis. How can you deliberately strengthen those bonds to provide better avenues of mutual encouragement? If you can't think of anyone, pray and ask the Holy Spirit to show you someone you can perhaps cultivate a relationship with. Once you have at least one person in mind, think through a practical way to make contact with that person.

LESSON 9

TOPIC

How To Construct a Wall of Defense, Part 3

SCRIPTURES

1. **1 Peter 5:9** — Whom resist stedfast in the faith, knowing that the same afflictions are accomplished in your brethren that are in the world.

2. **Psalm 119:164** — Seven times a day do I praise thee because of thy righteous judgments.

3. **James 3:16** — For where envying and strife is, there is confusion and every evil work.

GREEK WORDS

1. "resist" — **ἀνθίστημι** (*anthistemi*): to stand against; to stand in opposition; it demonstrates the attitude of one who is fiercely opposed to something and therefore determines to do everything within his power to resist it; to stand against it; to withstand; to defy; militarily, it was used to depict a preplanned resistance; to arrange oneself against; to strategically oppose; an orderly and planned resistance

2. "stedfast" — **στερεός** (*stereos*): to bolster; to reinforce

3. "confusion" — **ἀκαταστασία** (*akatastasia*): originally, it described thorn bushes or prickly plants; it depicted something that causes pain when someone becomes ensnared in it; it eventually described situations filled with disorder, disturbance, or trouble; disorder or disruption that results in upheaval of any sort; any type of instability or confusion, personal, organizational, governmental, or political

4. "evil" — **φαῦλος** (*phaulos*): terribly bad; exceedingly vile; something worthless; foul, ugly, offensive; something that is in a miserable state or condition

SYNOPSIS

Many years ago when we bought our big church building in Moscow, we had to reinforce it. As it was, the building was a little shaky and weak. But then we wrapped all the columns and walls in steel and bolstered the building. Now the building is so strong that if we wanted to, we could add on additional floors. What began as somewhat weak is now exceedingly strong because we *reinforced* it. That is what this Greek word *stereos* — translated "stedfast" — means in First Peter 5:9. And this is what we are to do with our faith.

The emphasis of this lesson:

Acknowledging God and learning to say no are two more ways to strengthen your defensive wall.

The Fifth Brick of Defense: Every Day, Stop and Acknowledge God

As we mentioned in lesson 7, King David was surrounded with a lot of injustice. He had enemies on the outside. He had enemies in his own family. He had enemies in his palace. Yet rather than be emotionally swamped by all the attacks — by all the things that could potentially happen to him — he said in Psalm 119:164, "Seven times a day do I praise thee because of thy righteous judgments." David was saying, "Acknowledging God is something I strategically choose to do seven times a day."

When I first read that verse, I thought "I'm going to do that." So I tried to figure out a way to stop seven times a day and just acknowledge God's control in my life. So I said, "Okay I'll acknowledge God at 8:00 a.m., at

10:00 a.m., 12:00 p.m., and so on. I had a whole plan, and I was constantly trying to remember to do it. Well, although I'm in constant fellowship with God throughout my day, it was a challenge to remember every designated time I was supposed to stop and acknowledge the presence of God. So one of my sons said, "Dad, let me help you." He set up an alarm on my cellphone that chimes throughout the day. And guess what? Every time it chimes — it doesn't matter if I'm in the car, if I'm in the meeting, or wherever I am — I pause momentarily and say, "Jesus, You are Lord. I recognize Your presence. You are here with me. You are justice. You are in control."

Do you know what that does? It helps me mentally fortify myself. The thoughts of injustice or the attacks of the enemy against my mind can't penetrate because multiple times throughout my day, I'm deliberately reflecting on the fact that God is good, Jesus is Lord, and everything is going to be all right. Jesus is righteous regardless of any injustice that's happening around me. And this helps me. It helps me build a wall of defense mentally to keep the devil out of my thoughts and out of my life.

This is something that you can do as well. Just put an alarm on your phone that rings several times a day, and let it remind you to acknowledge the presence of God. In fact, this method has become such a fixture in my life that now when my phone chimes, the people who are with me know what I do. So guess what they do? They join me! They throw their arms up and say, "Amen, Lord. We recognize Your presence." It helps all of us keep up a wall of defense as we acknowledge that Jesus really is Lord.

The Sixth Brick of Defense: Every Day, Say No to the Things You're Not Supposed To Do

This might be the most difficult one to do. But it is so important because when you say yes to everything you hear — and to every possibility and request that is presented to you — it will eventually lead to confusion and weakness. If you're saying *yes, yes, yes* all the time, chaos will come to your schedule, your mind, your finances, and your mind and emotions. And that confusion will lead to strife and unrest because you simply cannot do it all. Then you throw the door open to the devil.

James 3:16 says, "For where envy and strife is, there is confusion and every evil work." That word "confusion" is the Greek word *akatastasia* and, originally, it described thorn bushes or prickly plants. Well, you wouldn't want to get caught in that! This word depicted something that causes pain when someone becomes ensnared in it. It describes situations filled with disorder, disturbance, or trouble — disruption that results in upheaval or any type of instability or confusion, including personal, organizational, governmental, or political. This is something that is thorny, something that hurts. It *ensnares* you.

The word "evil" in James 3:16 is the Greek word *phaulos*, which literally means *terribly bad, exceedingly vile, something worthless, foul, ugly, offensive, something that is in a miserable state or condition.* When you get into confusion, it opens the door to every foul, ugly thing. And I guarantee you that if you're saying yes to everything that comes down the pike, you're going to get into confusion, and you're probably going to get into strife — strife with yourself, strife with others, strife with your schedule, etc.

I'm sure you don't want to experience this kind of fallout, so you're going to have to learn to say no. When you say no to the things you're supposed to say no to, you are strengthening your wall of defense. You're bolstering and reinforcing yourself spiritually and mentally.

It is a fact that 85 percent of what you regularly do, someone else can do, and 10 percent of what you regularly do, someone else can be trained to do. That leaves 5 percent of what you regularly do that only *you* can do. So let me ask you: Are you focusing on the 5 percent that is only what you can do? Or are you consumed with the 95 percent that others could do or help you do?

Many years ago, I used to conduct all our staff meetings. I was involved in every decision in the ministry. The ministry just kept getting bigger and bigger, and I felt guilty if I didn't attend every meeting and be part of every decision. I felt like I had to be everywhere and be a part of every conversation. I truly thought that's what it meant to be a responsible leader.

But then I had a health crisis. I couldn't keep up with the growing ministry. Guess what I had to learn? Just what I mentioned above: that 85 percent of what I was doing, I didn't need to do. Someone else could do it. And, really, there was another 10 percent of what I was doing that others could be trained to do. The truth was, about 5 percent of what I was doing was my contribution, and that was really what I needed to focus on. So I rearranged my life. I gave away the 85 percent. Then I trained someone else for the 10 percent. And I began to focus on the 5 percent that was my personal contribution.

When I did that, things really began to happen. When I let other people do all those other things, they began to succeed because suddenly they were no longer under my control. They could function without me having to be a part of everything. I also began to succeed and flourish in the real gifts God had given to me, which was about 5 percent of all that I had been doing.

What about people who are constantly coming to you with requests, saying, "I need you to contribute to this" or, "I need you to take this job" or, "I need you to volunteer for this"? In the early years in the Soviet Union, people came to me for financial contributions all the time. People thought I had resources even if I did not, and because everyone around me was basically poor, I felt obligated to say yes to everything. So I said, "Yes, I'll help. How can I not say yes?"

Do you know what happened? Exactly what I'm telling you. I got into confusion. And I got into strife. I got into confusion because I'd said yes to so many things, I couldn't keep track of them. I got into strife with myself and with our finances because it was just a mess saying yes all the time. We didn't have enough money to pay for all the things I had said yes to out of guilt. I had to learn that it's just smart to say no to the things you're supposed to say no to.

Also, if you say yes to everything, you're robbing someone else of a blessing because there was someone else who was supposed to say yes instead of you. And if you had said no, that other person would have shown up to say yes and step into their area of responsibility. You robbed someone else of what they were supposed to do because you felt you had to say yes to everything. You need to learn that it's wise to say no at times.

I've even had to learn to say no to myself. I'm a fountain of ideas — I have a new idea every day! But every idea I have is not divine. And I've had to learn to say, "Rick, all of your ideas are not divinely inspired." And because I have men in my life who speak to me, they hear my ideas. And they tell me when they think one is a *God* idea or just *my* idea. That extra accountability helps me learn what to say yes to and what to say no to.

Saying no to the things you're supposed to say no to is very important. It will keep you from getting into confusion. It will stop you from getting into strife with yourself, your schedule, your finances, etc. — with all the things that concern you and affect your life.

STUDY QUESTIONS

> Study to shew thyself approved unto God, a workman that needeth
> not to be ashamed, rightly dividing the word of truth.
> — 2 Timothy 2:15

1. Search for the word "confusion" in different versions of the New Testament. Write a brief summary of what you find. Why is confusion something you want to avoid?

2. Find three different examples of New Testament saints acknowledging God and His matchless presence (e.g., John the Baptist, Peter, Mary, etc.). What did each saint say about God and why?

PRACTICAL APPLICATION

> But be ye doers of the word, and not hearers only,
> deceiving your own selves.
> — James 1:22

1. Write "My Life" on the top of a page and make three columns below it. Label the first column 85 (for the tasks anyone can do), the second column 10 (for the tasks others can be trained to do), and the third 5 (for the tasks that only you can do). Prayerfully ask the following questions:

   - What am I doing that someone else could be doing?
   - Is there someone I can train to do some of the things I'm doing?
   - How can I spend more time doing the things only I can do?

LESSON 10

TOPIC

Sealing the Cracks in Your Life

SCRIPTURES

2. **Ephesians 5:18-21** — And be not drunk with wine, wherein is excess; but be filled with the Spirit; Speaking to yourselves in psalms and hymns and spiritual songs, singing and making melody in your heart

to the Lord; Giving thanks always for all things unto God and the Father in the name of our Lord Jesus Christ; Submitting yourselves one to another in the fear of God.

3. **Revelation 3:1-3** — And unto the angel of the church in Sardis write; These things saith he that hath the seven Spirits of God, and the seven stars; I know thy works, that thou hast a name that thou livest, and art dead. Be watchful, and strengthen the things which remain, that are ready to die: for I have not found thy works perfect before God. Remember therefore how thou hast received and heard, and hold fast, and repent. If therefore thou shalt not watch, I will come on thee as a thief, and thou shalt not know what hour I will come upon thee.

GREEK WORDS

1. "filled" — **πληρόω** (*pleroo*): to fill to capacity; to fill to the full

2. "psalms" — **ψαλμός** (*psalmos*): songs of praise

3. "hymns" — **ὕμνος** (*humnos*): sacred compositions, the primary goal of which is to give glory and honor to God

4. "spiritual songs" — **ᾠδαῖς πνευματικαῖς** (*odais pneumatikais*): songs in the spirit; singing in the spirit; singing in tongues

5. "melody" — **ψάλλω** (*psallo*): to pluck the strings of a harp or bow; a heartfelt expression of music

6. "submitting" — **ὑποτάσσω** (*hupotasso*): pictures obedience to authority; submission to authority in any context; one who is under authority; to defer to someone else

7. "watchful" — **γρηγορέω** (*gregoreo*): to be on your guard, to be watchful, or attentive; it primarily denotes the watchful attitude of one who is on the lookout to make certain no enemy or aggressor successfully gains entry into his life or place of residence; to be on high alert; it depicts a person whose attitude is to never let up; to be watchful, wide awake, to make certain a sinister force doesn't sneak up to overtake

8. "strengthen" — **στηρίζω** (*steridzo*): to make fixed and solid, like a column that holds up the roof of a house; to brace, to shore up, to bolster, to support, or to uphold; it fundamentally describes the act of reinforcing and supporting

9. "remember" — **μνημονεύω** (*mnemoneuo*): a word that denoted a written record used to record and memorialize a person's actions; it

often signified a statue, monument, or some type of memorial that was intended to be permanent; to remember, recollect, mention, commemorate, or to memorialize

10. "repent" — **μετανοέω** (*metanoeo*): a change of mind that results in a complete, radical, total change of behavior; a decision to entirely turn around in the way that one is thinking, believing, or living; a decision to change one's thinking, believing, or actions; a total transformation affecting every part of a person's life, both inside and outside, resulting in a behavioral change

SYNOPSIS

The ancient city of Sardis was once the capital of the Lydian kingdom, and it eventually became a big city in the Roman province of Asia. This was a very rich and powerful walled city, but history shows that over a period of time, its citizens became rather smug about who they were, and complacency began to set in. They thought, *We're great. We're rich, mighty, powerful, and renowned. No one can ever hurt or affect us.* But little by little, the city of Sardis began to fall into disrepair. Too smug to notice, they became vulnerable to enemy intruders.

Apparently, that's what happened to the Sardis church as well, because in Revelation chapter 3, Jesus spoke to this church and said, "You have a name. You have a reputation that you're alive. But the truth is, you're nearly dead" (*see* Revelation 3:1) They were living in a shadow of their former spiritual glory, and Christ told them repent.

Repentance is often the solution to problems in our lives — to make a decision to change, to go back where we once were spiritually, and to do what is right before God.

The emphasis of this lesson:

Finish your wall of defense by keeping filled with the Holy Spirit, and practice repentance to keep cracks from forming.

The Seventh Brick of Defense: Every Day, Pray To Be Refilled With the Holy Spirit

In Ephesians 5:18-21, the apostle Paul wrote, "And be not drunk with wine, wherein is excess; but be filled with the Spirit; Speaking to yourselves in psalms and hymns and spiritual songs, singing and making melody in your heart to the Lord; Giving thanks always for all things unto God and the Father in the name of our Lord Jesus Christ; Submitting yourselves one to another in the fear of God."

Being refilled with the Holy Spirit is something we need to do on a daily basis. Paul began in this passage by saying, "Be not drunk with wine." The word "drunk" describes a person who is a drunkard; he is inebriated. When a person is drunk, he does not think or act soberly. He drops his guard, saying and doing things he wouldn't normally do and permitting things he wouldn't normally permit. So when Paul said, "Be not drunk with wine," he was actually telling us to be sober — the same thing Peter said in First Peter 5:8 when he wrote: "Be sober, be vigilant…."

Paul said that instead of drunkenness, believers should be "filled with the Spirit." The word "filled" here is from the Greek word *pleroo*. It means *to fill to capacity or to fill to the full*, and the Greek tense really means *be BEING filled* with the Spirit.

This means that every day, you can be refilled with the Holy Spirit. Yes, there is an initial experience of being filled with the Holy Spirit. But from that moment forward, your goal should be *to keep being filled* with the Holy Spirit.

Every day when I wake up, I pray for a fresh infilling of the Holy Spirit. It takes seconds to pray that, but the result is monumental. When you're refilled with power, refilled with inspiration, and refilled with divine energy, it changes everything. It changes the way you think, and it makes you less susceptible to attack.

According to Ephesians 5:19, you are to be so filled with the Spirit that you're speaking to yourself in "…psalms and hymns and spiritual songs, singing and making melody in your heart to the Lord." That word "psalms" is the Greek word *psalmos*. It means *songs of praise*. The word "hymns" — the Greek word *humnos* — describes *sacred compositions* or *music with a primary goal to give glory to God*.

So rather than thinking about yourself and your dilemma, these kinds of songs and hymns will keep you focused on God and on His goodness and glory. "Spiritual songs" is from the Greek *odais pneumatikais*, which really means *songs in the spirit, singing in the spirit*, or *singing in tongues*. And the word "melody" (*psallo*) means *to pluck the strings of a harp or a bow*. It describes the heartfelt expression of music on an instrument.

This passage describes a person not down in the dumps, but one so filled with the Holy Spirit that he's singing songs, hymns, and spiritual songs. He's singing in tongues, filled to overflowing with the Spirit of God. In other words, an overflow takes place. His mind and emotions are affected. He is just so filled with Holy Spirit.

Well, that person doesn't make a very good target for the devil to take down! Even if the enemy tried to penetrate that person's life, it would be a challenge for the kingdom of darkness because that person is so filled with presence and glory of God.

Then Ephesians 5:20 begins with "Giving thanks." It's very hard to be negative when you're filled with thanksgiving. And here the Bible says that when you're filled with the Holy Spirit, you're also filled with thanksgiving.

Finally, verse 21 says, "…Submitting one to another.…" The word "submitting" — the Greek word *hupotasso* — literally means *to be in submission or to defer to someone else*. When you're filled with the Holy Spirit, you're in a position to be helped because you're willing to be helped — you allow others to be those "allied troops" in your life.

Again, here are our seven bricks of defense:

1. Every day, spend time with God in the morning. (Psalm 5:3)
2. Every day, spend time feeding your spirit on other sources. (2 Timothy 4:13)
3. Every day, spend some amount of time in quietness. (Proverbs 27:19; Psalm 46:10)
4. Every day, spend some amount of time with those who strengthen you. (Hebrews 10:25)
5. Every day, take time throughout your day to acknowledge God. (Psalm 119:164)
6. Every day, say no to the things you're not supposed to do. (James 3:16)
7. Every day, pray for a fresh infilling of the Holy Spirit. (Ephesians 5:18-21)

If you'll do these seven things, you will build a wall of defense that will make it extremely difficult for the devil to get into your life. Even if he tries to attack you, he won't get in because you have built a barricade. You've been vigilant — diligent and on high alert. You've taken precautionary, preplanned, steps to make sure the devil never gets inside.

Be Sure To Repent and Seal the Cracks in Your Life

Now let's talk a little more about city of Sardis and the church there that Christ told to repent (*see* Revelation 3:1). According to history, Sardis was a very ancient city surrounded by thick, high walls and set on the peak of a mountain (an acropolis). It was reputed to be a city *that could not be penetrated.*

But the people of Sardis became smug about their security, and they actually began to say, "We are the city that will never fall. Because of where we're located on the top of a mountain, and because of our thick, high walls, we can never be penetrated by an enemy."

But they'd become so smug about how invincible they were that they didn't notice how, geologically, things were changing. The earth was moving, and over a long period of time, the walls of the city began to form cracks. These cracks did not appear abruptly; they showed up very slowly. But because the citizens were so smug about how secure they were, they weren't paying attention to their foundations, which had begun to shift. And through negligence — through simply ignoring their foundations — their walls were forming cracks.

Then one day, an enemy came and discovered those cracks. And the enemy, who could never penetrate the city before, figured out that now they could slip into the city through the ever-broadening cracks. So one night while the people of Sardis were sleeping, Persia came. They scaled the cliffs up to the base of the city, and one by one, the enemy began to slip through the cracks and into Sardis. The next morning when the people of Sardis were awakened, they were shocked to find they were surrounded by an enemy on the inside!

But that did scenario did not have to take place! If the city of Sardis had been paying attention instead of being negligent, they would have recognized those forming cracks. But because they weren't looking diligently, they allowed those cracks to form and then become wide enough to allow an enemy to creep in.

This makes me think again of Peter's words in First Peter 5:8, in effect: "Be vigilant. Put up a wall of defense because the devil the adversary is looking for a gaping hole. And if you have a sealed-up wall, he's looking for a crack — any little entry point through which to slither into your life."

And what did Jesus say to the church of Sardis? He told them, "Things with you are not so swell. You've become weakened, and you need to strengthen the things that remain. You need to deal with your issues, with places of neglect" (*see* Revelation 3:1, 2). Then in verse 3, Jesus said, *"Repent."*

The word "repent" is the Greek word *metanoeo*, and it describes *a change of mind that results in a complete, radical, total change of behavior.* It means *a decision to entirely turn around in the way that one is thinking, believing, or living.* Repentance produces a transformation affecting every part of a person's life — both inside and outside — resulting in behavioral change.

Jesus said to the church of Sardis, "My friends, you have issues because of negligence. You need to deal with the cracks in your foundation because the devil has been penetrating your ranks. Now it's time for you to recognize what needs to change and do something about it."

Notice Jesus never just says, "Recognize your error" or, "Just say you're sorry" or, "Admit you made a mistake." No, Jesus told that church to *repent.* Repentance is the action that closes the door. Repentance seals the cracks. Repentance changes things.

If you've discovered you have a gaping hole in the wall around your life, it's time to repent. Maybe that opening formed through negligence, disobedience — or maybe it was because of something done accidentally or ignorantly. Nevertheless, there was a violation of some principle, and that breakdown yielded an entry point for the adversary to wage an attack. Repentance will close the door and seal the cracks, so if you know the devil has gained access to your life, you can stop the access! You stop it through the act of repentance.

This ten-lesson series will really make a difference for you if you'll do something with it. You can recognize the enemy's modes and methods and operation — and you can absolutely build a wall around your life that will barricade and keep him at bay from yourself and everything you hold as precious. And you can do this *starting today!*

STUDY QUESTIONS

**Study to shew thyself approved unto God, a workman that needeth
not to be ashamed, rightly dividing the word of truth.
— 2 Timothy 2:15**

1. Even if you don't consider yourself musical, Ephesians 5:18-20 says everyone is to make music to the Lord. Find two or three examples of people throughout the Bible who did that, and write them down. What were there situations these people found themselves in? What was their outcome?

2. The idea of repentance mentioned in Revelation 3 is found throughout the Bible. Find at least three other verses about repentance. Using these verses, write a summary that answers these two questions: a) how does repentance work? and b) why is it so important?

PRACTICAL APPLICATION

**But be ye doers of the word, and not hearers only,
deceiving your own selves.
— James 1:22**

1. Make a list of the seven bricks that comprise your wall of defense. Place it where you can see it every day as a reminder to practice these things regularly until they become a habit.

2. In your time with God in the morning, ask the Holy Spirit to help you sing a spiritual song. It may just start out with one word (in English or in other tongues), but give voice to it and let it flow out of your innermost being.

3. Is there any area of your life you may be smug or prideful about? Ask the Holy Spirit to bring any such areas to your attention so you can repent and keep those places off-limits to the enemy.

A Prayer To Receive Salvation

If you've never received Jesus as your Savior and Lord, now is the time for you to experience the new life Jesus wants to give you! To receive God's gift of salvation that can be obtained through Jesus alone, pray this prayer from your heart:

Jesus, I repent of my sin and receive You as my Savior and Lord. Wash away my sin with Your precious blood and make me completely new. I thank You that my sin is removed, and Satan no longer has any right to lay claim on me. Through Your empowering grace, I faithfully promise that I will serve You as my Lord for the rest of my life.

If you just prayed this prayer of salvation, you are born again! You are a brand-new creation in Christ! Would you please let us know of your decision by going to **renner.org/salvation**? We would love to connect with you and pray for you as you begin your new life in Christ.

Scriptures for further study: John 3:16; John 14:6; Acts 4:12; Ephesians 1:7; Hebrews 10:19,20; 1 Peter 1:18,19; Romans 10:9,10; Colossians 1:13; 2 Corinthians 5:17; Romans 6:4; 1 Peter 1:3

Notes

Notes

CLAIM YOUR FREE RESOURCE!

As a way of introducing you further to the teaching ministry of Rick Renner, we would like to send you FREE of charge his teaching, "How To Receive a Miraculous Touch From God" on CD or as an MP3 download.

In His earthly ministry, Jesus commonly healed *all* who were sick of *all* their diseases. In this profound message, learn about the manifold dimensions of Christ's wisdom, goodness, power, and love toward all humanity who came to Him in faith with their needs.

☑ **YES, I want to receive Rick Renner's monthly teaching letter!**

Simply scan the QR code to claim this resource or go to: **renner.org/claim-your-free-offer**

Connect

WITH US!